CONSIDER SUCH BEAUTIFUL AND MEANINGFUL NAMES AS:

*Shango—the god of storms, thunderbolts and lightning

*Malindi—a fifteenth-century African kingdom that traded with China

*Neema—Swahili for "Divine Favor"

*Candace—the name of five strong ancient Ethiopian queens

*Ellison—Ralph Ellison wrote the landmark novel *Invisible Man*

*Ar...

What To Name Your African American Baby

BENJAMIN FAULKNER

ST. MARTIN'S PAPERBACKS

929.4 FAU

WHAT TO NAME YOUR AFRICAN-AMERICAN BABY

Copyright © 1994 by Benjamin Faulkner.

All rights reserved. No part of this book may be used or reproduced in any manner whatsoever without written permission except in the case of brief quotations embodied in critical articles or reviews. For information address St. Martin's Press, 175 Fifth Avenue, New York, N.Y. 10010.

Library of Congress Catalog Card Number: 94-25777

ISBN: 0-312-95449-2

Printed in the United States of America

St. Martin's Press trade paperback edition/October 1994
St. Martin's Paperbacks edition/June 1995

10 9 8 7 6 5 4 3 2 1

*I dedicate this book, with love, to Marylin Brannock.
But always, give God the glory.*

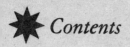 *Contents*

INTRODUCTION   xi

1. CONTEMPORARY NAMES   1

2. AFRICAN-AMERICAN HEROES AND HEROINES   9

   African-Americans Who Made a Difference   10
   Leaders in Government   19
   Organizational Leaders   25
   Educational Leaders   29
   Authors and Journalists   32
   Musicians and Dancers   37
   Actors and Actresses   43
   Artists   48
   Scientists   51
   Businesspeople   54
   Athletes   56

3. NAMES FROM AFRICA'S MAGNIFICENT HISTORY   62

   Queens   62
   Kings and Chiefs   64
   Goddesses   66
   Gods   67
   Rich Ancient Cities and Kingdoms   68

4. NAMES FROM THE VAST AFRICAN CONTINENT 72

Teeming Rivers   73
Magnificent Mountains   73
Grand Lakes   73
Modern African Countries and Major Cities   74

5. TRADITIONAL AFRICAN NAMES   78
AND THEIR DEFINITIONS

Swahili   80
Yoruba   82
Zulu   86
Hausa   88

6. UNIQUE NAMES FROM FOUR AFRICAN   90
LANGUAGES AND THEIR DEFINITIONS

Swahili   91
Yoruba   104
Zulu   122
Hausa   136

PRONUNCIATION GUIDE   151

BIBLIOGRAPHY   157

INDEX   159

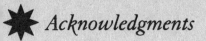 *Acknowledgments*

Conni Faiferlick, De'Andrea Bell, Suzanne Infantima, Fonda Burkett, Brian Wolfe, Simon Foster, Rebecca Crosby, Charlotte Olson, Chani Olson—and all my friends at Rock Bottom—thank you.

And thank you Jenny Notz, this book's editor at St. Martin's Press, for helping to make this a better book.

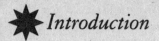# Introduction

Today's African-American parents are eagerly casting aside traditional American names in favor of names that demonstrate a proud respect for a rich, distinctive heritage. Written especially for African-American parents, *What to Name Your African-American Baby* exemplifies this creative spirit. In this book, you'll find a vast treasure chest of possible names for your child, every one of which can be given with love and pride.

A name is the first gift you give your child. The new little life in your care is a helpless bundle, but the direction that life takes will be influenced by the name you choose. Every new baby deserves a distinction and its own identity. The unique name that you select—one that has special meaning for you—will set forever the course of your baby's life.

Choose wisely.

Give your baby a great legacy to live up to.

To inspire you, this book discusses traditional African names as well as new naming traditions created by today's African-American parents. For names evoking those who have come before us, I point you toward celebrated African-American men and women, African kings and queens, gods and goddesses, magnificent ancient African kingdoms, as well as modern-day countries and cities. Additionally, I have chosen the areas of Africa where the ancestors of many African-Americans came from, taken the languages of those areas, Swahili, Zulu, Hausa, and Yoruba, and translated beautiful, descriptive English words into these languages to open up a continent of possible names.

You will find thousands of distinctive, original, and majestic names for your baby in this book. Enjoy your search.

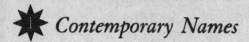

Contemporary Names

African-Americans are throwing out the old ways of naming a child and starting brand-new traditions by choosing contemporary names that reflect rich creativity on the part of parents.

In this chapter, you'll find some of those unusual and original names, and you'll read about the new naming traditions parents are coming up with—through the creation and selection of a name—to share the legacies of love and hope they have for their child.

Spell a traditional name in an unusual way, but retain the familiar pronunciation:

GIRLS

Traditional	New
Angie	ANJEY
Betty	BEHTY
Carol	KAROLE
Carrie	CAIREE
Darlene	DARLEINE
Fran	PHRAN

Traditional	New
Melissa	MELISSAH
Raquel	RAKEL
Sally	SALEE
Susan	SUZUN
Wanda	WANDAH

BOYS

Traditional	New
Adam	ADM
Bill	BIL
Douglas	DOUGLAHS
Harold	HAEROELD
James	JAIMS
Jesse	JESEY
Michael	MIKUL
Robert	ROBURT
Steve	STEEV
Tony	TOENEY

Add a new beginning to a name; for example, attach a syllable like *La, Wa, Ni, Sha, Tri,* or *Ja* to a traditional name:

GIRLS

Traditional	New
Andrea	LEANDREA
Anna	BREANNA
Dawn	LADAWN
Donna	LADONNA

Traditional	New
Ellen	TRIELLEN
Linda	WALINDA
Michelle	NISHELL
Rose	LEROSE
Shawna	SHASHAWNA
Sue	LASUE

BOYS

Traditional	New
Allen	TRIALLEN
Bill	SHABILL
Carl	TRACARL
Dan	NADAN
Dean	JADEAN
Grant	MOGRANT
Jaime	JAJAIME
Jay	DEJAY
Pat	SHAPAT
Tom	SHATOM

A traditional name with a syllable added to the end is what some clever parents have done:

GIRLS

Traditional	New
Ann	ANNRE
Barbara	BARBARASHA
Carol	CAROLSHAY
Claire	CLAIRKITA

Traditional	New
Gloria	GLORIYAE
Lisa	LISATA
Maggie	MAGGLEAN
Pam	PAMIA
Wanda	WANDAVISA
Yvette	YVETTEEN

BOYS

Traditional	New
Burt	BURTELL
Calvin	CALVINAH
Carver	CARVERSHO
Cleve	CLEVEN
Don	DONELL
Gary	GARYDEE
Jamaal	JAMAALDEEN
James	JAMESONE
Ken	KENSHAY
Lamont	LAMONTEL
Ray	RAVON

Create a new name by changing the first letter of a name:

GIRLS

Traditional	New
Catherine	JATHERINE
Diana	KIANA
Eva	IVA

Traditional	New
Karen	VAREN
Laura	TAURA
Mia	NIA
Nessa	DESSA
Paula	NAULA
Rebecca	TREBECCA
Sarah	VARAH
Yvonne	DVONNE

BOYS

Traditional	New
Adam	ODAM
Connelly	RONNELLY
Darryl	VARRYL
Donald	TONALD
Henry	GHENRY
Kevin	TEVIN
Louis	HOUIS
Oliver	ALIVER
Silas	MILAS
Tyrone	WYRONE

Using a word describing a characteristic that a parent wants to instill in a child is an old naming custom. Very often today, this method reflects turmoil or bad times in a parent's life and the hopes for a better future.

These names can be used for girls or boys:

CARE	CHASTITY
CHANGE	CHEERFUL

CHOICE	INNOCENCE
CONDOLENCE	JUDGMENT
COURAGE	PATIENCE
COURTESY	PIETY
DEARNESS	PRIDE
ELEGANCE	PROBITY
FORGIVENESS	RESOLUTION
FREEDOM	RESPECT
FUTURE	SÁGE
GIVING	SOBRIETY
GOODNESS	TENACITY
HONOR	VIRTUE

Samples of other descriptive words used as names:

GIRLS

BREEZE	STAR
JEWEL	SUNSHINE
QUEEN	WINDY

BOYS

CANNON	LAKE
CHASE	PRINCE
HAMMER	ROCK
ICE	SPIKE
KING	STORM

Three-syllable names beginning with *La* for girls are popular because they are soft-sounding. And there are a lot of two-syllable names beginning with *Ja* that are chosen for boys because they are strong-sounding. Here are some examples of both:

GIRLS

LA'ANDRA	LATASHA
LADONNA	LATIFAH
LANIVA	LATINA
LARITA	LATOYA
LASHAINA	LAVEENA
LASHANDRA	LAWANDA
LASHANTA	LAYVONNE
LATANDA	

BOYS

JAJU	JANTU
JAMAL	JARAIN
JAMIN	JAREEM
JAMON	JAVIN
JANAL	JAVO
JANEEL	

Unique names with a special significance to the family are invented when parents use a part of the mother's name and a part of the father's name. For instance, the name Dawnjohn is a combination of Dawn and John. Experiment with first and last names to find a combination that sounds appealing to you. Alternatively, begin your own tradition through the outright invention of a new name. Names created by African-American parents include:

GIRLS

ATIRA	SANTIEA
CHABRIS	SAVITA
CHANTE	SHAMLA
CHARMEE	SHANDY
CYANA	TENEE
DAVERA	THYRANN
JOSOYA	TOLANI
LELEEJAH	WENDAY
SALUDAE	ZETAY
SAMELLAA	

BOYS

BANTONE	KEYA
BARONE	LARENZ
BOUKMAN	RIDDICK
DAVON	SHARMBA
DAWIT	SHERLON
DELICE	TORR
DREE	TRANEY
GALLANE	TREVLIN
JOEZER	VINDON
KEELY	

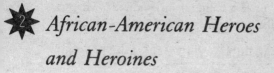

African-American Heroes
and Heroines

Your child can become an explorer of the universe or a pioneer in literature or a President of the United States. He or she can become an African-American who makes a difference in the world.

The tiny life in your care will grow into its own identity because of your love and nurturing. The name you give your child is the beginning. We've named our children after our heroes and heroines since civilization began in Africa. That hero or heroine can be your own father, or grandmother, or someone who figured prominently in your life. It doesn't have to be someone famous. Give your child a name that requires him or her to strive, to reach for something great inside.

This selection of African-Americans who have made a difference in our lives is a very small smattering of names from a long list of prominent African-Americans, pioneering African-Americans, and influential African-Americans. Some of their names are traditional; others are more unusual. But all reflect positively the achievement of African-Americans.

When you look at this list of famous African-Americans, let your imagination roam to come up with possible names for your child. For instance, a young friend of mine knows a boy proudly named Ellison, after the writer Ralph Ellison. Don't consider only the first name of your hero or heroine; the middle or last name of an admired predecessor can become a distinctive first name for your child.

AFRICAN-AMERICANS WHO MADE A DIFFERENCE

These African-Americans are just a few of those who have broken new ground and paved the way for others' successes.

Names for Girls

ALTHEA Gibson.   Tennis great Gibson became the first African-American to win a major tennis title. A winner at Wimbledon and the U.S. Open in 1957 and 1958, she was the number-one female player in the United States in 1957. Raised in Harlem, she began playing tennis in the street.

BESSIE Smith.   Known as the Empress of the Blues, she will remain one of the greatest blues singers of all time. She died from injuries she sustained in an automobile accident, and it was widely (but incorrectly) rumored she bled to death when no white hospital would admit her.

CLARA Hale.   After raising forty foster children, each of whom went to college, she founded Hale House in New York City. Hundreds of drug-addicted and AIDS babies have been cared for there. "Mother" Hale believed children were sent to her by God so she could surround them with love.

CONSTANCE Motley.   After arguing nine successful cases before the U.S. Supreme Court, she became the first

African-American woman to be appointed as a federal judge.

DIAHANN Carroll. This actress was the first African-American to star in her own television series: *Julia*.

ELIZABETH Duncan Koontz. Koontz was the first African-American president of the National Education Association (NEA).

GWENDOLYN Brooks. The first African-American to win the Pulitzer Prize, she received this international honor in 1950 for her book of poetry *Annie Allen*.

HARRIET Ross Tubman. After escaping slavery, Tubman helped three hundred family members and friends do the same as a "conductor" on the Underground Railroad. She served Abraham Lincoln as a Union spy and at one time had at forty-thousand-dollar bounty on her head. Known as the Moses of Her People, she deeply believed that faith in God and a strong family would lead African-Americans out of oppression.

IDA B. Wells Barnett. A fiery journalist and lecturer, she was exiled from the South for her crusade against lynching. Later, she helped to found the NAACP and organized the first African-American women's political organization, the Alpha Suffrage Club of Chicago.

JOSEPHINE Baker. As a cabaret performer in the 1920s and 1930s, she held the nightlife of Paris in the palm of her hand.

Queen LATIFAH.   Born Dana Owens, she is a pioneer in the male world of rap music, exposing hard social issues by presenting them in a more positive way than the male rappers before her.

LORRAINE Hansberry.   Her play, *A Raisin in the Sun*, made her the first African-American woman to have a play on Broadway, and the first African-American to win the New York Drama Critics' Circle Award for Best Play of the Year.

MAE Jemison.   In 1992, she became the first African-American woman in space.

MAGGIE Lena Walker.   She dreamed of a bank owned and operated by African-Americans. Her dream became reality in 1903 when Walker became president and founder of the St. Luke Penny Savings Bank in Richmond, Virginia, making her the first African-American woman bank president.

MAHALIA Jackson.   The world's greatest gospel singer: Everywhere she went, crowds of all ages and races surrounded her and cheered her singing and her message of civil rights. Jackson never had a music lesson, could not read music, and almost never sang a song the same way twice. And she never sang the Lord's music in a bar or nightclub.

MARIAN Anderson.   No African-American had performed at the White House before Anderson and no African-American before her was named a member of the

Metropolitan Opera Company. The first African-American diva, she toured the world for three decades.

MARY C. Terrell.   She helped found the Niagara Movement, which became the NAACP. Her work also helped ratify the Nineteenth Amendment, which gave women the right to vote.

MARY McLeod Bethune.   Presidents Coolidge, Hoover, Roosevelt, and Truman appointed Bethune to government posts, making her the first African-American woman to hold federal office. She founded the Daytona Normal and Industrial Institute for Negro Girls, which merged with Cookman Institute to become Bethune-Cookman College. Bethune's message to the world was that through education, children grow into greatness.

MAXINE Waters.   A congresswoman from an inner-city Los Angeles district, she grew to be considered the most influential black woman in the Democratic Party.

OPRAH Gail Winfrey.   As host and executive producer of *The Oprah Winfrey Show*, she has courageously and empathetically brought to the forefront of American consciousness dark taboos and deep social problems in an effort to find answers that will help heal American society.

ROSA Parks.   She is considered the Mother of the Civil Rights Movement because she refused to give up her seat on a bus to a white man. Later, she founded the Rosa and Raymond Parks Institute for Self-Development, which aims to empower youngsters through self-esteem.

SHARON Pratt Kelly.   As mayor of Washington, D.C., she became the first African-American woman to be elected mayor of a major American city.

SHIRLEY Anita Chisholm.   The first African-American woman elected to the United States Congress and the first African-American woman to run seriously for President of the United States.

SOJOURNER Truth.   Born Isabella Baumfree, she was a popular lecturer who served her people as a leading abolitionist and as an aid to slaves who had escaped to the North. She is today recognized as one of America's first and greatest advocates of the anti-slavery and women's rights movements.

Names for Boys

ADAM Clayton Powell, Jr.   Dynamic and exciting in the U.S. Congress, Powell was first elected to the House of Representatives in 1944 and represented his New York district for more than twenty years.

ALEX Haley.   This distinguished author's work included *The Autobiography of Malcolm X* and *Roots*, which encouraged interest in Africa and African-American genealogy. His awards included the National Book Award, a special Pulitzer Prize, and the NAACP Spingarn Medal.

BENJAMIN Banneker. In the 1700s, few African-Americans had the opportunity to be scientists, but Banneker overcame obstacles to become an astronomer, mathematician, clockmaker, surveyor, and champion for freedom. In his day, he was the most well-known African-

American in the country. George Washington recruited Banneker to help plan the city of Washington, D.C.

BILL (William) Cosby. Actor, author, director, producer, philanthropist, and spokesperson, Cosby has elevated the image of the black family and the self-respect of individual African-Americans. He promotes education as the means to getting ahead.

BOOKER Taliaferro Washington. An educator and writer, he helped to establish Tuskegee Institute at a time when African-Americans had few educational opportunities.

CHARLES Richard Drew. The first person to set up a blood bank. Drew made the world safer as a result of his work. Until he began studying how blood and blood plasma could be stored, very little was known about blood banks. Drew developed a process whereby blood plasma could be processed and preserved; in doing so, he saved thousands of lives during World War II and after.

COLIN Powell. He was the first African-American to become Chairman of the Joint Chiefs of Staff, the most important military post in the world.

DUKE (Edward Kennedy) Ellington. From his birthplace in Washington, D.C., and his home in New York City, Ellington became a symbol of American jazz to the entire world.

FREDERICK Douglass. He escaped slavery in the 1830s to become a prominent abolitionist, lecturer, and writer, and his advice and counsel was sought by Abraham Lincoln during the Civil War. Douglass founded, and edited for seventeen years, the *North Star*, an abolitionist newspaper pointing the way to freedom. He firmly believed that education was the answer to the economic problems of African-Americans.

GEORGE Washington Carver.   An agricultural chemist who discovered multiple uses for the peanut, sweet potato, and soybean, Carver was involved in pioneering research during the early 1900s that enabled farmers to diversify their crops, thereby transforming the economy of the South.

HANK (Henry) Aaron.   With more home runs than Babe Ruth, Aaron held the all-time record for home runs hit. He was one of the few African-Americans to become an executive with a major baseball team.

HOMER Plessy.   He refused to ride on the "colored" car, and in 1896 his celebrated case, *Plessy* v. *Ferguson*, challenging the concept of "separate but equal" segregation, went to the Supreme Court.

JACKIE (John Roosevelt) Robinson.   He played baseball with the Brooklyn Dodgers, thereby becoming the first African-American to play in the major leagues. Robinson was also the first African-American admitted to the Baseball Hall of Fame.

JAMES Weldon Johnson.   With his brother J. Rosamond Johnson, he wrote the song that would become the Black National Anthem, "Lift Every Voice and Sing." Johnson was also an esteemed poet and the author of *God's Trombones*, a work based on folk sermons.

JEAN Baptiste Point Du Sable.   He has been called America's greatest black explorer. With a keen mind and a sharp eye, Du Sable built his trading post and started the settlement that later became known as Chicago.

JESSE Jackson.   After heading Operation Breadbasket for the Southern Christian Leadership Council (SCLC) and People United to Save Humanity (PUSH)—Jackson's own organization, set up to create economic opportunities for African-Americans—Reverend Jackson ran for the Democratic nomination for President of the United States in 1984 and 1988. He is responsible for gaining thousands of jobs and business opportunities for African-Americans.

MALCOLM X.   Born Malcolm Little, this prominent leader of the Black Muslims and African-American pride movements also founded the Organization of Afro-American Unity.

MARCUS Garvey.   The most influential African-American leader during the early 1900s, Garvey founded the Universal Negro Improvement Association and fiercely promoted the Back to Africa movement.

MARTIN Luther King, Jr.   Dr. King gave his famous "I Have A Dream" civil rights speech before more than 250,000 people during the 1963 March on Washington. A prominent civil rights leader who advocated nonviolent resistance to segregation, his work helped influence Congress to pass the Civil Rights Act of 1964 and the Voting Rights Act of 1965. In 1964, Dr. King won the Nobel Peace Prize. On his tombstone are carved these words from his March on Washington speech: "Free at last, free at last, thank God Almighty, I am free at last."

MATTHEW Alexander Henson.   Possibly the first explorer to reach the North Pole, he guided Adm. Robert Peary's expedition. It was Henson who planted the American flag at the North Pole.

RALPH Bunche.   For his role as a mediator between the Arabs and Israelis, Bunche became the first African-American to win the Nobel Peace Prize.

ROBERT Abbott.   In his weekly paper, the *Chicago Defender*, he promoted the North as the promised land of opportunity and is almost single-handedly responsible for the mass exodus of African-Americans to the North.

THURGOOD Marshall.   The first African-American to serve on the United States Supreme Court, Marshall was appointed as a federal judge of the U.S. Second Circuit Court of Appeals by President Kennedy. Later, President Johnson asked Marshall to become one of the government's chief lawyers, the solicitor general of the United States. It was under Johnson that Marshall became a Supreme Court justice, a position he held until the beginning of President Clinton's term of office.

WILLIAM Edward Burghardt Du Bois.   After years as a lightning rod for civil rights, W. E. B. Du Bois cofounded the Niagara Movement in 1905, which later became the NAACP.

LEADERS IN GOVERNMENT

These heroic African-Americans have put their considerable skills to work as government officials.

Names for Girls

ANNA Arnold Hedgeman.   The first woman to serve in a New York mayoral cabinet, she spent many productive years in government.

BARBARA Jordan.   Former congressperson Jordan was the first African-American elected to the Texas Senate since 1883; she was the powerful keynote speaker at the 1992 Democratic National Convention.

CARDISS Collins.   From Illinois, Collins was the first African-American and the first woman to serve as Democratic whip-at-large.

CAROL Moseley-Braun.   Her victory in the 1992 Illinois senatorial race made Moseley-Braun the first African-American woman to be elected to the U.S. Senate.

CAROLYN Robertson Payton.   In 1978, she became the first African-American and the first woman to head the Peace Corps.

CARRIE Perry.   When elected mayor of Hartford in 1987, she became the first African-American female mayor of a major city.

DEBORAH Sampson. Disguised as a man, she served bravely in the Continental army and later became the first woman to collect a soldier's pension, which Paul Revere helped her secure.

EDITH Sampson. The first African-American woman appointed as official representative to the UN, she later became the first African-American woman elected as a circuit court judge in the United States.

ELEANOR Holmes Norton. Under President Carter, she became the first woman to head the Equal Employment Opportunity Commission.

GEORGIA Powers. The first African-American elected to the Kentucky state senate, she served for more than twenty years.

HAZEL O'Leary. O'Leary is the Secretary of Energy in President Clinton's cabinet.

JANE Bolin. America's first African-American woman judge to serve New York, she was on the bench for forty years.

JEWELL Jackson McCabe. McCabe is president of the National Coalition of 100 Black Women.

MARY Elizabeth Bowser. Born a slave, this incredible woman acted as a Union spy while working undercover in Jefferson Davis's Confederate White House.

MARY Frances Berry.   Teacher, historian, and author, she was appointed Civil Rights Commissioner by President Carter.

PATRICIA Harris.   As secretary of the Department of Housing and Urban Development under President Carter, she became the first African-American woman to serve as a presidential cabinet member.

SHERIAN Grace Cadoria.   This brigadier general became the highest-ranking African-American woman in the armed forces of the United States.

UNITA Blackwell.   She was Mississippi's first African-American female mayor.

YVONNE Brathwaite Burke.   In 1972, she became the first African-American woman ever elected to Congress from California.

Names for Boys

ANDREW Young.   Once an aide to Martin Luther King, Jr., he has served as mayor of Atlanta, congressman from Georgia, UN ambassador, and is now chair of the Atlanta Committee for the Olympic Games.

ARTHUR Mitchell.   Born to slave parents, he became an Illinois congressman and successfully argued his own case before the Supreme Court, winning a decision that declared Jim Crow laws illegal.

BLANCHE Bruce.   Elected Mississippi senator in 1874, this advocate of minority rights was the first African-American to serve a full term in the U.S. Senate.

CHARLES Rangel.   New York representative Rangel is a longtime and powerful member of the U.S. Congress.

CLARENCE McClane Pendleton.   Named chairman of the Civil Rights Commission by President Reagan, he was the first African-American to assume this post.

CLIFFORD Alexander.   The first African-American to serve as the secretary of the Department of the Army, he received that department's Outstanding Civilian Service Award.

COLEMAN Young.   He served five terms as mayor of Detroit.

DAVID Dinkins.   Dinkins was the first African-American mayor of New York City.

(Lawrence) DOUGLAS Wilder.   When elected governor of Virginia, Wilder became the first African-American governor in U.S. history.

EDWARD W. Brooke.   The first African-American elected senator since 1881, he served Massachusetts for two terms.

FREEMAN Bosley.   In 1993, he became the first African-American mayor of St. Louis.

GEORGE Thomas Leland.   This esteemed civil rights activist and U.S. congressman was killed in a plane crash on a U.S. mission near Ethiopia in 1989.

HAROLD Washington.   Washington was the first African-American mayor of Chicago.

LOUIS W. Sullivan.   Sullivan was the secretary of the Department of Health and Human Services under President Bush.

JOHN Conyers, Jr.   Long active in the Democratic Party, Conyers was elected U.S. congressman from Detroit.

JOSEPH Rainey.   In 1871, he became the first African-American member of the House of Representatives and served three terms.

KURT Schmoke.   After serving in President Carter's White House, he became the first African-American mayor of Baltimore.

MICHAEL White.   He was elected mayor of Cleveland.

MAYNARD Jackson.   After serving as mayor of Atlanta from 1974 to 1982, he was again elected to the position in 1989.

OSCAR De Priest.   In 1928, this Illinois Republican became the first African-American from the North to be elected to Congress.

ROBERT Smalls.   Named a pilot in the Union navy by President Lincoln, he ultimately became the only African-American to be promoted to captain during the Civil War; he was later elected to the U.S. Congress from South Carolina.

ROBERT Weaver.   The former director of the Department of Housing and Urban Development, he was the first African-American appointed to a presidential cabinet.

RONALD Brown.   The first African-American to lead a major political party, he was chairman of the Democratic National Committee and was later named Secretary of the Department of Commerce.

RONALD Dellums.   This longtime congressman became the first African-American chair of the House Armed Services Committee.

SIDNEY John Barthelemy.   After years of work with community organizations, he was elected mayor of New Orleans.

THOMAS Bradley.   He was the mayor of Los Angeles for twenty years.

WALTER Fauntroy.   A longtime civil-rights activist, he now represents the District of Columbia in Congress.

WELLINGTON Webb.   Webb was elected the first African-American mayor of Denver.

WILLIAM Henry Hastie.   Hastie was the first African-American to become a federal appeals judge.

Organizational Leaders

These people have devoted their time, energy, and talent to organizations dedicated to improving society, particularly for African-Americans.

Names for Girls

ALTHEA Simmons.   As chief congressional lobbyist for the NAACP, she was considered one of the best in her field.

BARBARA Harris.   In 1989, she was elected the first female bishop in the Episcopal Church, breaking more than four hundred years of tradition.

BERTHA Knox Gilkey.   Gilkey is an internationally known activist for welfare and tenants rights.

CORETTA Scott King.   The widow of Martin Luther King, Jr., she has continued his work for human rights.

DAISY Bates.   As Arkansas president of the NAACP, she was an instrumental force in the desegregation of Little Rock's Central High School.

DOROTHY Height.   Height served as the president of the National Council of Negro Women, founded by Mary McLeod Bethune.

ELLA Josephine Baker.   This devoted activist spent more than fifty years working for all the major civil rights organizations.

ENDESHA Ida Mae Holland.   Holland is a professor and playwright who has been jailed more than a dozen times while working in the civil rights movement.

ENOLIA McMillan.   In 1985, she became the first female president of the NAACP.

EVA del Vakia Bowles.   She devoted her life to the YWCA, believing this women's organization to be a successful proving ground for relations among the races.

FANNIE Lou Hamer.   The founder of the Mississippi Freedom Democratic party, she was one of the first African-American delegates at a Democratic National Convention.

FAYE Wattleton.   Wattleton was the first woman president of Planned Parenthood.

MARIAN Wright Edelman.   The first African-American woman admitted to the Mississippi bar, she is the founder and president of the Children's Defense Fund.

PAULI Murray.   A cofounder of NOW, she was a dedicated activist for women's and civil rights.

RAMONA Edelin.   She has been president of the National Urban Coalition since 1982.

SEPTIMA Poinsette Clark.   Affiliated with SCLC, the NAACP, and NOW, she was known as the Queen Mother of the civil rights movement.

Names for Boys

ASA Philip Randolph. A determined activist for both civil rights and organized labor, he helped to organize the 1963 March on Washington; New York City's A. Philip Randolph Institute continues his work.

BAYARD Rustin. Dedicated to nonviolence, he was one of the founding members of the SCLC and was director of the A. Philip Randolph Institute.

BENJAMIN Chavis. In 1993, he succeeded Benjamin Hooks as executive director of the NAACP.

BOBBY (Robert) Seale. Seale was a cofounder and former chairman of the Black Panther party.

CALVIN O. Butts. The pastor of New York City's Abyssinian Church, he has also taught university courses in urban affairs and black church history.

DANIEL Alexander Payne. A bishop in the African Methodist Church, he was a great educator and a powerful voice for emancipation.

ELDRIDGE Cleaver. The information minister of the Black Panther party, he is the author of *Soul on Ice*.

GARDNER Taylor. Baptist minister and community activist Taylor has worked with Martin Luther King, Jr., the Urban League, and recently on New York City's Board of Education.

JAMES Farmer.   Farmer was the founder of the Congress of Racial Equality (CORE), which first used Freedom Rides as a form of protest.

JOHN E. Jacob.   Jacob served as president of the National Urban League.

JOSEPH Lowery.   As president of the SCLC, he reinvigorated Operation Breadbasket's work for the economic empowerment of African-Americans.

MEDGAR Evers.   The violent death of this NAACP leader helped convince President John F. Kennedy to ask Congress for a comprehensive civil rights bill.

RALPH Abernathy.   A colleague of Martin Luther King, Jr., he served as president of the SCLC after King's death.

RANDALL Robinson.   He is the founder and director of TransAfrica, an organization devoted to lobbying Congress on issues involving Africa and the Caribbean.

ROY Wilkins.   This prominent newspaper editor was the executive director of the NAACP.

STEPHEN Gill Spottswood.   This bishop of the African Methodist Episcopal Zion Church and NAACP board member took on the Nixon administration for its policies toward African-Americans.

STOKELY Carmichael.   Now known as Kwame Toure, this civil rights activist and author popularized the concept of black power.

VERNON E. Jordan, Jr.   This former president of the National Urban League is now an adviser to President Clinton.

WHITNEY Young.   Young was a president of the National Urban League and a recipient of the Presidential Medal of Freedom.

EDUCATIONAL LEADERS

Realizing that education is the key to self-improvement, these inspirational African-Americans dedicated their lives to teaching.

Names for Girls

ANGELA Davis.   An educator and author, Davis was one of the most famous political activists of the 1960s and 1970s and is today recognized as a victim of political repression.

AUGUSTA Baker.   As a librarian, storyteller, and teacher, she provided guidance for generations of children.

BETTY Shabazz.   The widow of Malcolm X, she is an administrator at the City University of New York.

CHARLOTTE Hawkins Brown.   She founded the Palmer Memorial Institute, a college preparatory school for African-American students, when few other educational opportunities were available.

GLORIA Scott.   Now president of North Carolina's Bennett College, she was the first African-American female president of the Girl Scouts.

HALLIE Brown. Brown was Tuskegee Institute's first "lady principal."

JANIE Porter Barrett. In the early 1900s, she was the guiding force behind the Virginia Industrial Institute for Colored Girls, one of the first schools committed to the rehabilitation of African-American female juvenile delinquents.

JEWELL Plummer Cobb. For more than ten years, she has been president of California State University at Fullerton.

JOHNNETTA Cole. She became the first African-American woman president of Atlanta's Spelman College, a historically black women's institution.

LUCY Diggs Slowe. Slowe served as the first African-American woman dean of Howard University.

MARGUERITE Ross Barnett. In 1990, this distinguished educator became the first African-American and the first woman elected president of the huge University of Houston.

MARVA Collins. This famed teacher founded Chicago's Westside Preparatory School to educate the city's deprived children.

NIARA Sudarkasa. Born Gloria Marshall Clark, this internationally known anthropologist is president of the historic African-American college Lincoln University.

OLIVIA Davidson Washington. With her husband, Booker T. Washington, she founded Tuskegee Institute.

Names for Boys

ALAIN Locke.   A distinguished scholar and former chairman of Howard University's philosophy department, he introduced America to the Harlem Renaissance.

CARTER G. Woodson.   This author, scholar, and teacher is remembered as the Father of Modern Black History.

CLIFTON R. Wharton.   The first African-American president of the State University of New York, the nation's largest university system.

CORNELL West.   He has taught at Yale, Princeton, and now Harvard, and is author of the best-selling *Race Matters*.

FRANKLYN Jenifer.   Until 1994, Jenifer was president of his alma mater, Howard University.

FREDERICK Patterson.   Formerly of the Tuskegee Institute, he founded the United Negro College Fund.

HENRY Louis Gates, Jr.   He is chairman of Harvard University's African-American Studies Department and an author.

HOUSTON Baker.   He is a celebrated author, teacher, and literary critic.

JESSE Edward Moorland.   His private library grew into the first African-American research collection in a major American university, the Moorland-Spingarn Research Center at Howard University.

JOE Clark.   Immortalized in the film *Lean on Me*, this educator has been honored by the NAACP and the White House.

LEON Higginbotham.   He started out as a shoe porter; today he is a law professor at the University of Pennsylvania and a former judge.

MOLEFI Kete Asante.   Born Arthur Lee Smith, he is considered the founder of the Afrocentric Movement.

MORDECAI Johnson.   The first African-American president of Howard University, he held that position for more than thirty years.

WILLIAM H. Gray III.   This former congressman left government to become president of the United Negro College Fund.

AUTHORS AND JOURNALISTS

The potent words of these writers expand our minds and explain their times.

Names for Girls

ALICE Allison Dunnigan.   Dunnigan was the first African-American woman to be an accredited White House correspondent.

ALICE Walker.   Her third novel, *The Color Purple*, received both the Pulitzer Prize and the American Book Award.

CAROLE Simpson.   This television journalist can currently be seen on the ABC national news.

CHARLAYNE Hunter-Gault.   A journalist, she has written for *The New Yorker* and *The New York Times*; she is now a reporter for *The MacNeil/Lehrer Newshour*.

GLORIA Naylor.   Her stirring novels include *The Women of Brewster Place, Mama Day*, and *Bailey's Cafe*.

GWENDOLYN Bennett.   One of the best-known poets of the Harlem Renaissance, she was also a journalist and an artist.

LUCY Terry.   A slave who won her freedom, she is considered America's first black poet.

LORENE Cary.   Cary is the author of the memoir *Black Ice* as well as a writer for *Time, Newsweek*, and *Essence*.

MARGARET Walker Alexander.   This educator and author's work includes the poem, "For My People."

MAYA Angelou.   Acclaimed author, actress, and teacher, her celebrated works include *I Know Why the Caged Bird Sings*.

NTOZAKE Shange.   Poet, playwright, and novelist, she is best known for her choreopoem, *for colored girls who have considered suicide/when the rainbow is enuf.*

OCTAVIA Butler.   This award winner is one of the most popular and highly regarded science fiction writers.

PAULE Marshall.   Author of *Praisesong for the Widow* and numerous other books, she set the stage for African-American women authors such as Toni Morrison.

RITA Dove.   This writer and teacher won the 1987 Pulitzer Prize for poetry and was recently named the poet laureate of the United States.

SONIA Sanchez.   This activist, teacher, and award-winning author has written plays, poetry, short stories, and children's books.

SUSAN Taylor.   Taylor is the editor in chief of *Essence*.

TERRY McMillan.   Her books include *Mama, Disappearing Acts*, and the runaway best-seller *Waiting to Exhale*.

TONI Morrison.   This acclaimed author and editor has won the Pulitzer Prize, the National Book Critics' Circle Award, and the Nobel Prize for Literature.

VIRGINIA Hamilton.   Although she writes in a variety of genres, she is perhaps best known for her children's books.

ZORA Neale Hurston.   An anthropologist and writer, her best-known book is *Their Eyes Were Watching God*.

Names for Boys

AUGUST Wilson. This Pulitzer Prize and Tony Award–winning playwright's work includes *Fences* and *The Piano Lesson*.

BERNARD Shaw. A familiar face to all CNN viewers, he is this news network's chief Washington anchor.

BRYANT Gumbel. He is the longtime cohost of NBC's *Today Show*.

CARL Rowan. Rowan is a journalist and author; his nationally syndicated column is carried by newspapers around the country.

CLAUDE Brown. He wrote the best-selling autobiography *Manchild in the Promised Land*.

CHARLES Fuller. Fuller is the author of the Pulitzer Prize–winning *A Soldier's Play*.

CHARLES Johnson. He is the author of the National Book Award–winning *Middle Passage*.

EDWARD Bradley. This Emmy Award–winning journalist is a *60 Minutes* correspondent.

ELLIS Cose. Cose is a respected journalist, editor, and columnist.

ISHMAEL Reed. He is a well-known author and anthologist.

IMAMU Amiri Baraka (LeRoi Jones). This writer and teacher has been a leading spokesperson for black power.

JAMES Baldwin. Author of novels, essays, and plays, he is an important contributor to twentieth-century American literature.

JOHN Edgar Wideman.   This award-winning author's works include *Fever* and *Philadelphia Fire*.

LANGSTON Hughes.   A dominant force in the Harlem Renaissance, this acclaimed poet, novelist, and playwright helped to popularize the work of his fellow African-American authors.

MAX Robinson.   He was the first African-American network news anchor.

PAUL Laurence Dunbar.   Noted for his use of black dialect, he was the first African-American poet to gain national stature in the United States.

RALPH Ellison.   Author of the classic *Invisible Man*, he won the 1952 National Book Award.

RICHARD Wright.   His works include the classics *Native Son* and *Black Boy*.

THOMAS Sowell.   He is an economist and writer who preaches that African-Americans must rely on themselves and not on the government.

TONY (William Anthony) Brown.   Brown is a television journalist and commentator famed for his long-running PBS program *Tony Brown's Journal*.

WILLIAM Wells Brown.   This nineteenth-century author is believed to be the first African-American to publish a novel.

MUSICIANS AND DANCERS

These performing artists have set a standard that is admired throughout the world.

Names for Girls

ANITA Baker.   This beautiful soul singer has been honored with Grammy Awards, NAACP Image Awards, and American Music Awards.

ARETHA Franklin.   She is fondly called the Queen of Soul.

BILLIE Holiday.   Born Eleanora Fagan, she was one of the most influential jazz singers of all time.

CARMEN McRae.   She is one of the jazz world's most acclaimed singers.

DEBBIE Allen.   Allen is a stage and screen sensation, choreographer, and director.

DIANA Ross.   This legendary songstress rose to fame with the Supremes.

DIONNE Warwick.   She is a Grammy-winning singer.

ELLA Fitzgerald.   Fitzgerald is universally beloved as the First Lady of Song.

EMMA Hackley.   This singer and teacher devoted herself to promoting traditional African music and African-American musicians.

ERNESTINE Anderson.   Her unforgettable style made this jazz singer a favorite on tour with the big bands of the 1940s and 1950s.

EVA Jessye.   Celebrated choral director for the first Broadway production of *Porgy and Bess*, she also had her own group, the Eva Jessye Choir.

FLORENCE Mills.   One of the biggest musical stars of the jazz era, she was also a determined advocate for her people.

GAIL Hightower.   This respected classical musician has been named NAACP Outstanding Woman in the Arts.

GRACE Ann Bumbry.   An opera singer who began singing in a church choir, she took the world by storm as the first African-American to perform at the prestigious Wagner Bayreuth Festival.

JANET Collins.   This legendary dancer was the first African-American prima ballerina with New York's Metropolitan Opera.

JUANITA Hall.   This talented singer's awards include the Tony.

JESSYE Norman.   This internationally renowned opera diva is a graduate of Howard University.

JUDITH Jamison.   A dancer and choreographer, she rose to fame with the Alvin Ailey American Dance Theater.

KATHERINE Dunham. A recipient of the Kennedy Center Honors, this pioneer of modern dance introduced Americans to African and Caribbean influences.

KATHLEEN Battle. She is an acclaimed opera star.

LENA Horne. This dazzling entertainer's retrospective, *Lena Horne*, was the longest-running one-woman show on Broadway.

LEONTYNE Price. This opera singer's awards include the Presidential Medal of Freedom.

LESLIE Uggams. This Tony award-winning singer and actress was one of the first African-American entertainers to appear regularly on television.

LILLIAN Evanti. Perhaps the most overlooked classical singer of the early twentieth century, she starred in European opera houses in the 1920s.

NATALIE Hinderas. This internationally acclaimed pianist was one of the first African-Americans to gain prominence in the world of classical music.

NINA Simone. Known as the High Priestess of Soul, this best-selling singer has used her music to condemn racism.

ODETTA. This civil rights activist performs the traditional songs of African-Americans throughout the world.

PEARL Bailey.   She began her career singing with Count Basie's orchestra, moved to stage and screen, and was ultimately named special adviser to the United States Mission to the United Nations.

SARAH Vaughan.   The Divine began her career at amateur night at Harlem's Apollo Theater; later, her signature voice made her one of the world's top jazz singers.

SIPPIE Wallace.   Known as the Texas Nightingale, she was a blues singer and songwriter.

VANESSA Williams.   The first African-American to be named Miss America, she now has a successful recording career.

WHITNEY Houston.   One of the biggest musical stars of the 1980s, she recently began an acting career.

Names for Boys

ALVIN Ailey.   An internationally celebrated dancer and choreographer, he was the founder of the Alvin Ailey American Dance Theater.

ANDRÉ Watts.   Watts is one of the most gifted pianists in the United States.

ARTHUR Mitchell.   This dancer and choreographer founded the famed Dance Theater of Harlem.

BEN Vereen.   Broadway fans love this Tony Award–winning actor, singer, and dancer.

BILL ("Bojangles") Robinson.   This legendary dancer's many roles included the lead in *Harlem's Heaven*, the first talkie with an entirely African-American cast.

BRANFORD Marsalis.   This talented saxophonist moved into the public eye as the *Tonight Show*'s bandleader.

CHARLIE Parker.   This influential jazz musician inspired the screen biography *Bird*.

CHARLES Mingus.   His compositions are some of the best in the history of jazz.

COUNT (William) Basie.   His famous jazz band was considered one of the world's best.

CURTIS Mayfield.   His songs, including "People Get Ready," are some of the most memorable of the civil rights era.

DEXTER Gordon.   This talented saxophonist received an oscar nomination for *Round Midnight*.

DON Cornelius.   He was the host and producer of *Soul Train*.

ERIC Dolphy.   A master of the alto sax and the bass clarinet, he toured with many jazz greats.

GEOFFREY Holder.   The talented Holder won two Tonys, including the best director award, for *The Wiz*.

GREGORY Hines.   An actor and dancer, he recently dazzled Broadway audiences in *Jelly's Last Jam*.

HARRY Belafonte.   Celebrated as a singer, he is also known as an actor and civil rights activist.

JIMI Hendrix.   Hendrix was an unforgettable rock guitarist and songwriter.

JOHN Coltrane.   This innovative saxophonist was a leading figure in jazz until his untimely death from cancer in 1967.

IRA Aldridge.   One of the leading Shakespearean actors of the nineteenth century, he was denied the opportunity to perform in the United States at the peak of his success.

LOUIS Armstrong.   Master of the trumpet and the big-band sound, he was one of the most influential musicians of all time.

MARVIN Gaye.   Gaye was a best-selling singer.

MILES Davis.   He was a genius trumpet player.

OTIS Redding.   A music star with his own record company, he died tragically in a plane crash but will be forever remembered for such songs as "(Sittin' on) the Dock of the Bay."

QUINCY Jones.   He began his career as a jazz trumpeter and is now a legendary producer.

ROY Eldridge.   Known as Little Jazz, this singer, drummer, and trumpeter was one of the great figures in music.

SAMMY Davis, Jr. This multitalented actor, singer, dancer, and comedian remains a legend in the entertainment world.

SCOTT Joplin. Joplin was the king of ragtime.

SMOKEY (William) Robinson. This singer, songwriter, and producer became one of Motown's biggests stars.

STEVIE Wonder. Born Steveland Judkins, he is a musical genius and social activist.

THELONIOUS Monk. His jazz compositions, including "Round Midnight," are classics.

WYNTON Marsalis. Cofounder of the Lincoln Center Jazz Ensemble, he is one of the finest jazz trumpeters of his time.

ACTORS AND ACTRESSES

On the big and little screens and in theaters, these talented African-Americans have entertained and enlightened millions of Americans.

Names for Girls

ANGELA Bassett. She was an Academy Award nominee for *What's Love Got to Do With It*.

BEAH Richards. This celebrated actress was nominated for an Academy Award for her role in *Guess Who's Coming to Dinner*.

BEVERLY Johnson.   Model turned TV personality, she was the first African-American woman to grace the cover of *Vogue*.

BUTTERFLY (Thelma) McQueen.   Outspoken against discrimination—at great cost to her own career—she will be forever remembered for her role as Prissy in *Gone With the Wind*.

CAROLE Gist.   In 1990, she became the first African-American to be crowned Miss USA

CICELY Tyson.   Her heroic and award-winning performances include roles in *The Autobiography of Miss Jane Pittman* and *Sounder*.

DOROTHY Jean Dandridge.   For her role in the all-black musical *Carmen Jones*, she became the first African-American to be nominated for an Academy Award for Best Actress.

HALLE Berry.   Berry is a model and actress whose films include *Boomerang* and *Jungle Fever*.

HATTIE McDaniel.   The first African-American woman to win an Academy Award, she was named Best Supporting Actress for her role in *Gone With the Wind*.

JASMINE Guy.   An actress, she has played Whitley Gilbert on television's *A Different World*.

JOIE Lee.   Lee has appeared in her brother Spike's *She's Gotta Have It* and *Mo' Better Blues*.

JULIE Dash.   As a filmmaker (*Daughters of the Dust*) she focuses on presenting the concerns of African-American women.

MARSHA Warfield.   A comedienne and actress, she starred in television's *Night Court*.

MOMS (Jackie) Mabley.   Born Loretta Mary Aiken, she performed regularly at Harlem's Apollo Theater and became America's first widely known African-American comedienne.

PHYLICIA Rashad.   This talented actress is perhaps best known as Claire Huxtable on *The Cosby Show*.

RUBY Dee.   An actress well known for her work with her husband, Ossie Davis, she is also a committed civil rights activist and poet.

WHOOPI Goldberg.   Born Caryn Johnson, this Oscar-winning actress and comedienne is committed to social change.

Names for Boys

BILLY Dee (William December) Williams.   He is known both as a talented actor and a romantic leading man.

CHRIS Rock.   Rock is a comedian, actor, and featured performer on *Saturday Night Live*.

DANNY Glover.   This talented actor has appeared on television, on stage, and in films including *Lethal Weapon* and its sequels.

DENZEL Washington.   This Academy Award winner is one of the most sought-after actors working today.

EARLE Hyman.   This distinguished actor is perhaps most recognized for his role on *The Cosby Show*.

EDDIE Murphy.   Murphy is a big box-office actor and entertainer.

FLIP (Clerow) Wilson.   In the 1970s, he became the first African-American to have a weekly prime-time television show bearing his own name.

FREDERICK O'Neal.   A cofounder of the American Negro Theater, he was the first African-American president of Actors Equity.

JAYE Davidson.   Davidson was the actor who surprised us in *The Crying Game*.

JAMES Earl Jones.   A winner of the Tony Award and the Drama Desk Award, he was also the voice of Darth Vader in *Star Wars*.

JOHN Singleton.   Singleton is the screenwriter and director who gave us *Boyz N the Hood*.

LA VAR Burton.   Burton played the lead in Alex Haley's *Roots*.

LAURENCE Fishburne.   This actor has received national recognition for his roles in *Boyz N the Hood* and *What's Love Got to Do With It*.

LOUIS Gossett, Jr.   He won an Oscar for his role in *An Officer and a Gentleman* and his performance in *Roots* garnered him an Emmy.

MARIO Van Peebles.   The actor and filmmaker who brought us *New Jack City*, among other films, he is the son of director Melvin Van Peebles.

MESHACH Taylor.   Taylor's acting credits include television's *Designing Women*.

MONTEL Williams.   Williams is a television talk-show host and former motivational speaker.

MORGAN Freeman.   This actor's work includes much-praised roles in *Driving Miss Daisy* and *Glory*.

PAUL Robeson.   The son of a runaway slave, he was a singer, actor, lawyer, athlete, and champion of human rights.

REDD Foxx.   Foxx is best known for his portrayal of Fred Sanford on television's *Sanford and Son*.

RICHARD Pryor.   He is known as a groundbreaking comedian, actor, writer, and Grammy winner.

SIDNEY Poitier.   He was the first African-American to win an Academy Award for Best Actor, for his performance in *Lilies of the Field*.

SPIKE Lee.   This filmmaker has brought us such groundbreaking movies as *Do the Right Thing* and *Malcolm X*.

WESLEY Snipes.   He began his career on Broadway and is now one of the hottest actors in Hollywood.

ARTISTS

Their contributions to the world of art and design are some of the most important in American history.

Names for Girls

ANN Lowe.   This fashion designer's most famous creation is the gown worn by Jacqueline at her wedding to John F. Kennedy.

AUGUSTA Savage.   She overcame discrimination to become one of America's most distinguished sculptors and promoters of African-American artists.

BARBARA Chase-Riboud.   A distinguished artist who employs African symbols in her work, she recently became an award-winning author.

CAMILLE Billips.   This respected sculptor and printmaker is also an award-winning filmmaker.

CLEMENTINE Hunter.   Considered one of America's most important folk artists, she never received any formal training.

MARY Edmonia Lewis.   Lewis is believed to be the first African-American female artist.

ELIZABETH Catlett.   After being refused admittance to an all-white art school, she graduated from Howard

University and is today one of America's most collected African-American sculptors.

ELIZABETH Keckley. This amazing woman bought her freedom, built a sewing business, and became official dressmaker and companion to First Lady Mary Todd Lincoln.

MARGARET Burroughs. The founder of Chicago's Du Sable Museum of African-American History, she is also one of America's most honored African-American artists.

NORMA Merrick Sklarek. Sklarek was the first nationally recognized African-American female architect.

PHOEBE Beasley. An admired artist whose work has been exhibited worldwide, she is also the first African-American to be named president of American Women in Radio & Television.

SELMA Burke. This award-winning sculptor and teacher's many creations include the sculpted portrait of FDR that appears on the dime.

Names for Boys

AARON Douglas. The most important painter of the Harlem Renaissance, he completed portraits of such notables as Mary McLeod Bethune.

BEAUFORD Delaney. A gifted painter, his work includes many portraits of notable African-Americans.

BYRON Lars.   This up-and-coming fashion designer was named Rookie of the Year for 1991 by *Women's Wear Daily*.

CHARLES Alston.   The work of this talented muralist adorns the facade of Harlem Hospital in New York.

EDWARD Spriggs.   The founder of Harlem's Studio Museum, a cultural center for the African-American community, he was a forerunner in the celebration of Kwanzaa.

GORDON Henderson.   A fashion designer, his work has been snapped up by Saks Fifth Avenue.

GORDON Parks.   Author, composer, and filmmaker, Parks is perhaps best known for his photography.

JAMES Van Der Zee.   He was an internationally recognized photographer whose work captures early twentieth-century Harlem life.

JOHN Lankford.   The first African-American architect on record, he built the Pythian Building in 1901 with a team comprised entirely of African-Americans.

PAUL Revere Williams.   The first African-American to become a member of the American Institute of Architects.

ROMARE Beardon.   His unforgettable collages are among the world's best known.

STEPHEN Burrows.   This celebrated fashion designer was a pioneer in his field.

SCIENTISTS

Their success in the fields of medicine and technology have improved our lives.

Names for Girls

ALEXA Canady.   She became the first African-American female neurosurgeon in the United States.

ALICE Woodby McKane.   She founded and presided over Savannah's first black-run healthcare center, then moved to Liberia where she established the country's first hospital.

BESSIE Coleman.   Less than twenty years after the Wright Brothers made their first successful flight, she was the first African-American woman to earn a pilot's license.

DORIS Wethers.   Wethers, an eminent pediatrician, is a leader in the fight to combat sickle-cell anemia.

DOROTHY Brown.   Brown was the first African-American woman surgeon in the South and a dedicated humanitarian.

HELENE Gayle.   A leader in AIDS research, she strongly believes it is important to make a contribution to the world.

JANE Wright.   Working at the Harlem Hospital research center founded by her father, she made many of the first important advances in cancer chemotherapy.

JUSTINA Ford.   Known as "Denver's Baby Doctor," she became Colorado's first black female physician and its best-known obstetrician.

MARY Mahoney.   She was the first African-American professional nurse.

MAY Edward Chinn.   Although she did not finish high school, this outstanding African-American was accepted at Columbia University and went on to practice medicine in Harlem for more than fifty years.

REBECCA Cole.   In the 1860s, she dared enter a medical field dominated by white males and was a practicing physician for more than fifty years.

REBECCA Lee.   Lee was America's first African-American female physician.

SHIRLEY Ann Jackson.   A MIT graduate, this physicist is one of America's most distinguished young scientists.

Names for Boys

ARTHUR Logan.   He devoted his medical career to Harlem Hospital and ultimately headed New York City's Council Against Poverty.

BENJAMIN Carson.   A miracle-working physician, he is the director of pediatric neurosurgery at Johns Hopkins Hospital.

DANIEL Hale Williams. This heart surgeon founded Provident Hospital, open to all, when other Chicago hospitals refused to employ African-American doctors.

DAVID Blackwell. This esteemed mathematician was the first African-American to be elected to the National Academy of Sciences.

FREDERICK McKinley Jones. A total of sixty-one patents were issued in this scientist's name; his inventions include the first automatic refrigeration system for trucks.

GARRETT Morgan. His inventions include the Morgan inhalator (later made into the gas mask) and the automatic traffic signal.

GRANVILLE T. Woods. Although he left school at ten, his many inventions include the Synchronous Multiplex Railway Telegraph, used to prevent train accidents.

GUY (Guion) Bluford. Bluford was the first African-American in space.

LEWIS Latimer. This celebrated inventor was a member of Thomas Edison's research team.

W. MONTAGUE Cobb. For many years a member of the Howard University Medical School and the NAACP, he was the first African-American president of the American Association of Physical Anthropologists.

PERCY Julian.   In the early part of the nineteenth century, he overcame discrimination to become one of the nation's leading chemists.

ROLAND Scott.   A medical pioneer, he spent fifty years at Howard University researching sickle-cell anemia.

RONALD McNair.   McNair was one of the astronauts aboard the ill-fated space shuttle *Challenger*.

SAMUEL L. Kountz.   This surgeon made medical history when he worked on the first kidney transplant between humans who were not twins.

WARREN Washington.   This ecologist is a much-sought-after expert on the "Greenhouse Effect."

BUSINESSPEOPLE

These business leaders and entrepreneurs have achieved success in areas historically closed to African-Americans.

Names for Girls

CAMILLE Cosby.   The wife of Bill Cosby, she is chief executive of Cosby Enterprises and a firm supporter of African-American educational institutions.

ERNESTA Procope.   Procope founded the nation's first African-American-owned insurance-brokerage agency.

JOAN Murray.   The first major African-American television news correspondent, she is also the founder of a successful advertising agency.

NAOMI Sims.   This businessperson and former model graces New York City's Naomi Sims Beauty Products, Limited.

SARAH Breedlove McWilliams Walker.   Her hair products company enabled her to become America's first self-made female millionaire and a noted philanthropist.

XERONA Clayton.   The first African-American woman to have her own television show in the South, she is now an executive with the Turner Broadcasting System, Inc. (TBS).

Names for Boys

BERRY Gordy, Jr.   Gordy founded Motown Records, the most successful African-American-owned recording company in history.

CLARENCE B. Jones.   He is chairman of Inner City Broadcasting, the owner of the large black newspaper, *Amsterdam News*.

GEORGE Johnson.   Johnson founded Johnson Products, the first company under African-American ownership to trade on the American Stock Exchange.

JOHN H. Johnson.   His company, Johnson Publishing, founded *Ebony* and *Jet* magazines.

JONATHAN Rogers.   As president of CBS Television Stations Division, he holds one of the most powerful positions in network television.

KENNETH I. Chenault.   He is president of American Express Consumer Card Group, USA.

PAUL Cuffe.   One of the wealthiest African-Americans of the eighteenth century, he made his fortune as a ship captain and later repatriated thirty-eight free black Americans to Sierra Leone.

PERCY Sims.   Formerly an elected official in New York State as well as a director of the Urban League and the NAACP, this attorney founded the Inner City Broadcasting Corporation.

REGINALD Lewis.   When he bought TLC Beatrice International Holdings, he became the owner of the largest African-American owned company in the United States.

ROBERT Johnson.   Johnson founded the Black Entertainment Television cable network.

T. THOMAS Fortune.   He founded the National Negro Business League with Booker T. Washington, and later the leading black journal *New York Age*.

WALLACE Amos.   Formerly a prominent talent agent, he went on to found the Famous Amos Chocolate Chip Cookies.

ATHLETES

The abilities and achievements of these African-Americans inspire us.

Names for Girls

ALICE Coachman.   Her 1948 performance in the high jump made her the first African-American woman to win an Olympic gold medal.

ANITA DeFrantz.   This 1976 Olympic medalist became the first African-American member of the Olympic Committee.

DEBI Thomas.   She was first African-American woman to win an Olympic medal in figure skating.

FLORENCE Griffith-Joyner.   This track star won four medals (including three golds) at the 1988 Olympics.

GAIL Devers.   A gold medalist at the 1992 Barcelona Olympics, she is currently considered the fastest woman in the world.

JACKIE Joyner-Kersee.   She was a gold medalist in the heptathalon and long jump at the 1988 Olympics.

NELL Jackson.   An Olympic athlete herself, she became the first African-American woman to serve as head coach to the women's Olympic track and field team.

WILMA Rudolph.   At the 1960 Rome Olympics, she became the first American woman to win three gold medals at track and field.

WYOMIA Tyus. The first winner of the gold medal for the one-hundred-meter race in two consecutive Olympic Games.

ZINA Garrison. Garrison is known as one of the world's best tennis players.

Names for Boys

ARTHUR Ashe. Ashe is universally admired and re-membered for his brilliant tennis, his courageous fight against AIDS, and his work for social change.

ART Shell. He is head coach of the Los Angeles Raiders.

BILL Russell. One of the finest players in the history of basketball, he led the Boston Celtics to eleven NBA championships.

CHARLES Barkley. This member of the Phoenix Suns was named the most valuable player in the NBA for the 1992–1993 season.

CLYDE Drexler. He is a professional basketball player with the Portland Trail Blazers.

CECIL Fielder. Fielder plays professional baseball.

DAVE Winfield. This professional baseball player went to the 1992 World Series with the Toronto Blue Jays.

DENNIS Green. He is head coach of the Minnesota Vik-ings.

FRANK Robinson. A tremendous baseball player, he made history as the first African-American manager in the major leagues.

GEORGE Foreman. A professional boxer, Foreman is now an actor.

HERSCHEL Walker. Walker is a professional football player.

JACK Johnson. Between 1910 and 1915, he reigned as the first African-American heavyweight boxing champion.

JACKIE Robinson. This Hall of Famer was the first black player in Major League Baseball.

JAMES Brown. This football player turned movie star was voted Football Back of the Decade for 1950–1960.

JESSE (James Cleveland) Owens. One of the world's first great track and field athletes, he triumphed at the 1936 Olympic Games.

JOE Louis. Louis was a heavyweight champion for more than eleven years, a world record.

JULIUS ("Dr. J.") Erving. This Basketball Hall of Famer led the Philadelphia 76ers to an NBA championship.

KAREEM Abdul-Jabbar. Born Lewis Ferdinand Alcindor, Jr., this basketball star led the L.A. Lakers to five NBA championships.

KIRBY Puckett.   Puckett, only five foot eight inches tall, plays professional baseball. His career with the Minnesota Twins includes two World Series crowns.

LEE Elder.   He was the first African-American golfer to earn one million dollars on the professional circuit.

MAGIC (Earvin) Johnson.   He is an AIDS activist and former basketball star.

MARSHALL W. Taylor.   Known as "Major," this cyclist was the first African-American U.S. National Champion and a favorite of President Theodore Roosevelt.

MICHAEL Jordan.   Famed basketball star turned baseball player, he is a hero to millions around the world.

MIKE Singletary.   He played twelve years with the Chicago Bears.

MUHAMMAD Ali.   One of the most famous boxing champions in the world, he changed his name from Cassius Clay.

O. J. (Orenthal James) Simpson.   This athlete turned actor and commentator was one of the best running backs in professional football.

PATRICK Ewing.   Ewing is a well-known basketball star.

REGGIE (Reginald) Jackson.   Jackson is a Baseball Hall of Famer.

SATCHEL (Leroy Robert) Paige.   This pitcher was a baseball superstar before the integration of the sport.

SHAQUILLE O'Neal.   The Orlando Magic center is known as the Shaq to his many fans.

WALTER Payton.   He rose to fame as a running back for the Chicago Bears.

WILLIAM White.   When this former All-Star became president of baseball's National League, he assumed one of the most important positions in sports.

WILLIE Mays.   This baseball Hall of Famer hit more than six hundred home runs for the San Francisco Giants.

WILLY T. Ribbs.   Ribbs was the first African-American to qualify for the Indianapolis 500.

✷ Names from Africa's Magnificent History

Go back through your own education. How much did you learn about the grand African empires and kingdoms? Most of us were shown pictures of naked natives and grass huts. But that is not the true picture of African royalty.

Bustling, vibrant city-states rich with commerce and learning have thrived and prospered, one after another, in Africa since the dawn of civilization.

While Europeans were trekking to the outhouse, one African kingdom had indoor plumbing in every house. Another had splendid armored knights on horseback riding proudly over the African plains.

Why not name your child after a great African kingdom or prosperous city-state, or after an African warrior king, or Africa's most prominent goddess?

You can give your child greatness straight out of African history.

QUEENS

AMANIRENAS.   She was the Cushite queen who fought the invading armies of Augustus Caesar, forcing the Romans to withdraw.

AMENIRDA.   She was queen of Thebes during the last part of the eighth century B.C.

ISMENIE.   Ismenie was Makeda's mother.

MAKEDA.   The queen of Sheba, she was a great builder, administrator, and international stateswoman who ruled along the Nile for fifty years.

NEFERTITI.   The most admired woman of her time, she was beautiful, intellectual, and driven by a great sense of purpose.

SHENAKDAKHETE.   She was the first independent Queen of Meroë.

SHEPENOUPET.   Shepenoupet was the last Cushite queen of Thebes.

SHEPENEPOUT.   Prophetess of Amon, she was also queen of Thebes.

TIYE.   She reigned for half a century as influential queen of the most powerful nation on earth in her time.

Triumphant Queens of Ancient Egypt

AHMOSE-NEFERTERE   MUTEMWIA
AHOTEP   NEITH-HOTEP
ANCHNESMERIR   NITOCRIS
MER-NEITH   SOBEKNOFRU
                        TA-WSRET

African Warrior Queens

CANDACE.   This is the name of five strong ancient Ethiopian queens.

CLEOPATRA.   A shrewd political maneuverer and a powerful voice for Egypt, she came to the throne at age eighteen.

YAA ASANTEWA.   She led the Yaa Asantewa war against the British in Ghana when the men of her country wouldn't.

HATSHEPSUT.   She is called the first queen in the history of mankind.

KAHINA.   She drove Arab armies out of her country in the sixth century in her effort to save Africa for Africans and thwart the spread of Islam.

TINUBU.   A great Nigerian warrior, she fought the slave trade.

NZINGHA.   Possessing both charm and ruthlessness, she fought off the Portugese invasion of her country, Angola, and, along with it, the Portugese slave trade. The most important personality in Angola for forty years, she preferred to be called a king.

KINGS AND CHIEFS

AGAJA.   He was king of Dahomey, on the coast of West Africa, in the early 1700s.

ASKIA MUHAMMAD TORE (also known as ASKIA THE GREAT). He ruled the mighty empire of Songhai in the sixteenth century.

DLAMINI. He was the founder of the royal clan of the Swazi people.

IMHOTEP. A prime minister during the Third Egyptian Dynasty, he is remembered today for the construction of the first pyramid.

KIMERA. Kimera was Kintu's great-grandson and a king of Buganda.

KINTU. He was the first ruler of Buganda. Myth has it that he and his son are guardians against wrong.

MUTESA. The thirtieth monarch of Buganda, he is famed for his competence and ambition.

NGWANE. A Swazi king, he led his people away from the coast and into the forests.

NZINGA A KNUWU (Nzinga Mbemba). He was king of the Congo in the 1500s.

OBA. He was the absolute monarch of Benin.

ODUDUWA. Oduduwa was considered the first king of Ife and the forefather of its people.

ORANYAN. Son of Oduduwa and a great warrior, he was the second king of the Yoruba of Nigeria.

OSAI TUTU.   The fourth king of the Ashanti, he ruled unyieldingly in the eighteenth century.

SAMORI IBU LAFIYA.   He bravely resisted the French invasion of West Africa.

SEKOU TORE.   He was a courageous leader in the Republic of Guinea's intense struggle for independence.

SHAKA.   This great Zulu king was born an unwanted child of what was considered a shameful union, but he rose to build a huge army that conquered vast territories of Africa.

SHAMBA.   A king of the Congo who sought to be the wisest of men, he is considered a great thinker and inventor.

SUNDJATA.   A powerful chief, he carved an empire out of the jungle near the Upper Niger.

TRUDO AUDATI.   This monarch had two titles: King of Dahomey and Emperor of Popo.

GODDESSES

ALA.   The Mother of Earth among the Ibo people of eastern Nigeria, she was one of the most important goddesses in Africa.

ISIS.   Looked upon as the source of Egypt's prosperity, she was the dominant goddess of ancient Egypt.

HATHOR. A goddess who succeeded Neith as Great Mother, she was the donor of life and the protector of the dead.

NEITH. Legend has it that Neith was self-begotten and self-produced; she is the oldest of all gods and an early example of the Great Mother.

YASAN. This was the name for the goddess of the wind.

GODS

AMMA. The one God, he was considered the creator of the people of Mali.

DONGO. Among the people of the Upper Niger, he was known as the god of storms.

ESHU. One of God's messengers, he was considered a guardian of human beings.

KIBUKA. He was the Bugunda war god.

LEZA. This was the name people in Central Africa used for Supreme Being.

MAWU. Mawu and his female counterpart, Lisa, were together believed to be the primeval twin creators.

MULUNGU. This was the name used by people in East Africa for God, or Supreme Being; the Creator of All.

MUSA.   He was the god of hunting.

NGEWO; MAWU; AMMU; OLORUN; CHUKWU.
These were the names used by the people of western Africa
for the Supreme Being.

NYAMBE.   People in all areas of the tropics used this
name for the Creator.

OGUN.   He was the god of iron.

OLOKUN.   The owner of the sea, he was the god of all
the great waters.

OLORUN.   He was the owner of the sky.

OSANYIN.   This was the name for the god of healing.

SHANGO.   He was a god of storms, thunderbolts, and
flashes of lightning.

TANO.   Tano was god of water among the people of
Ghana and the Ivory Coast.

ZIN-KIBARU.   A river spirit, he ruled over the fishes
and animals of the rivers.

RICH ANCIENT CITIES AND KINGDOMS

These beautiful and majestic place names may be given to
either a boy or a girl. Enjoy the sound of them when
deciding which name is right for your new child.

ASHANTI.   Ashanti was a home to sculptors who created and treasured ancient religious art.

AXUM.   While Islam was spreading across the African continent during the fifth century, this ancient Ethiopian kingdom remained a stronghold for Christianity.

BENIN.   Its king lived in a palace larger than many towns.

BORNU.   For more than two hundred years, fierce Bornu horsemen armored like European knights roamed the Sudan with defiant pride.

CUSH.   This was a highly civilized kingdom along the ancient Nile.

DJENNÉ.   This city was an important religious and educational center of the western Sudan.

GAO.   A large city, it was filled with rich African merchants, an abundance of gold, and a glamorous palace for the king and his court.

KATUNGA.   Katunga was a capital city on the edge of the rain forest.

KILWA.   While most civilized Europeans still believed the world was flat, this small island fortress had already developed ties to faraway China.

KUMASI. The capital of Ashanti, an economic empire deep in the Akan forest, it was so advanced, it had built-in plumbing long before Europe did.

KUMBI-SALEH. Located on the fringe of the great Sahara, this was the capital of the Ghanaian empire.

MALI. During the fourteenth century, Mali's rulers dazzled the Europeans with African pomp and circumstance.

MALINDI. In 1415, this African kingdom sent giraffes to China as a gift.

MEROË. Founded 560 years before the birth of Christ, Meroë was the capital city of the kingdom of Cush.

SONGHAI. This was a city of powerful kings who took pride in its advanced scholarship.

TIMBUKTU. The intellectual capital of the western Sudan, Timbuktu had so many scholars that merchants made more money from books than from any other commodity.

ZIMBABWE. It was a mysterious town surrounded by massive stone walls, behind which were the temple homes of divine rulers.

Other Significant Historic African Cities

BENGUELA	DONGOLA
BILMA	GHIAROU
BRAVA	GONDAR
DJANET	JENNÉ

KANO	SOFALA
LUANDA	TAGHAZA
MALINDI	TAKEDDA
MANAN	TETE
NIANI	TUNIS
RUFISQUE	ZEILA
SIJILMASA	ZUILA

Kingdoms of the Congo

ANGOI	CACONGO
ANGOLA	CONGO
BENGUELA	LOANGO

Old Kingdoms of the Guinea Region: The Ivory, Gold, Slave, and Delta Coasts of Africa

ABEOKUTA	IGBO
ABOMEY	ILORIN
ACCRA	JAQUIN
ARDRA	KETA
ASANTE	KUMASI
BEYIN	LAGOS
DAHOMEY	OIDAH
DENKYIRA	OPOBO
ELMINA	OYO
FANTE	WARRI
IBADAN	

✳ Names from the Vast
African Continent

Africa, the Dark Continent: If Africa is the birthplace of mankind, this is where God put Adam and Eve.

Rising out of the jungles and savannas, then swallowed by crackling barren deserts, civilizations were born, prospered, and folded, just like the cycle of crops. In the end, a spade turns them over into the earth. Then the earth is ready for the next civilization.

Africa's long history lies at the bottom of its lakes and stretches to the peaks of its mountains. They have endured and they have cradled the buried evidence of great African civilizations.

Parents in Africa and in the United States may name their children after a mountain range or a river or a city because the city means something special, or the river is important to the family, or the top of the mountain is where the child was conceived.

Some of the names in this section are majestic, like the voice of God; some are beautiful to the ear. They are a gift from the African continent to your child.

TEEMING RIVERS

BENUE	OKAVANGO
CUANGO	ORANGE
CUNENE	SANAGA
GAMBIA	SENEGAL
JUBA	SHABEELLE
KASAI	UBANGI
LIMPOPO	UELE
LUALABA	VAAL
NIGER	ZAIRE
NILE	ZAMBEZI

MAGNIFICENT MOUNTAINS

CAMEROON	KIRINYAGA
ELGON	MERU
EMI KOUSSI	THABANA-NTLENYANA
KARISIMBI	TOUBAKAL
KILIMANJARO	

GRAND LAKES

ALBERT	TANA
CHAD	TANGANYIKA
KARIBA	TURKANA
MWERU	VICTORIA
NYASA	VOLTA
RUKWA	

MODERN AFRICAN COUNTRIES AND MAJOR CITIES

ALGERIA: ALGER
                    CONSTANTINE
                    LAGHOUAT
                    ORAN

ANGOLA: LOBITO
                    LUANDA
                    MALANJE

BENIN: PARAKOU

BOTSWANA: GABORONE
                    SEROWE

BURKINA FASO: BOBO-DIOULASSO
                    OUGADOUGOU

CAMEROON: DOUALA
                    YAOUNDÉ

CENTRAL AFRICAN   BAMBARI
   REPUBLIC: BANGUI

CHAD: MOUNDOU
                    N'DJAMENA

CONGO: BRAZZAVILLE

DJIBOUTI: DJIBOUTI

EGYPT:	ASWÂN
	CAIRO
EQUATORIAL GUINEA:	BATA
ETHIOPIA:	ASMARA
	JIMA
GABON:	LAMBARÉNÉ
GHANA:	ACCRA
	KUMASI
	TAKORADI
GUINEA:	CONAKRY
	KANKAN
GUINEA-BISSAU:	BISSAU
IVORY COAST:	ABIDJAN
	BOUAKÉ
	YAMOUSSOUKRO
KENYA:	KISUMU
	NAIROBI
LESOTHO:	MASERU
LIBERIA:	MONROVIA
LIBYA:	SABHA
	TRIPOLI

MALAWI:	ZOMBA
MALI:	BAMAKO
	TOMBOUCTOU
MAURITANIA:	NOUAKCHOTT
MOROCCO:	CASABLANCA
	MARRAKECH
	RABAT
MOZAMBIQUE:	BEIRA
	MAPUTO
	LICHINGA
NAMIBIA:	TSUMEB
	WINDHOEK
NIGER:	NIAMEY
	ZINDER
NIGERIA:	IBADAN
	KANO
	LAGOS
	NGURU
	ONITSHA
SENEGAL:	DAKAR
SIERRA LEONE:	FREETOWN
SOMALIA:	HARGEISA

SOUTH AFRICA:	PRETORIA
SUDAN:	JUBA
	KASSALA
	KHARTOUM
SWAZILAND:	MBABANE
TANZANIA:	ZANZIBAR
	MWANZA
	TABORA
	TANGA
TOGO:	LOMÉ
UGANDA:	GULU
	KAMPALA
WESTERN SAHARA:	AD DAKHLA
	LAAYOUNE
ZAIRE:	KINSHASA
	KISANGANI
	LUBUMBASHI
	UBUNDU
ZAMBIA:	CHIPATA
	KABWE
	LUSAKA
ZIMBABWE:	BULAWAYO
	HARARE
	KARIBA

5 Traditional African Names and Their Definitions

Thousands of years ago, boys and girls in Africa were given names that had a meaning relevant to their village or city. Everyone had to learn to do something that would help ensure the prosperity of the community, and children were named according to the trade or task they would learn, or named according to the characteristic their parents most wanted them to adopt.

Then, over the centuries, three basic methods for choosing a name evolved.

The first naming tradition looks at the circumstances surrounding the child's birth. For instance, was the child born during a war? Was the child born at harvest time or at planting time? There are names that in English mean each of those circumstances; for example: He was born during a period of great strife; He was born after the harvest; She was born during the dry season.

The second naming method calls for a name that describes the state of the house or the state of the parents' relationship at the time of the birth, such as the name that translates: Born after parents separated.

Finally, in keeping with the ancient tradition, names are chosen to indicate what the parents hope the child will become. These may be names of virtue, like the name meaning patience, or the name of a trade, like the name meaning woodcarver.

Among some Africans today, a name is selected while the baby is crying. A list of names is read out loud to the baby and when it stops crying at a particular name, that is the name the baby has chosen.

Some names represent the deity the family worships. For instance, if the family worships the god of rain, the baby's name will have some relationship to this god. The intention is to help convince the god to look favorably upon the family or the child, or to ward off evil spirits.

Names have also been chosen to represent heroic deeds of the father or heroic deeds the parents see their child accomplishing in the future.

Certain cultures give a baby a name based on the day of the week it is born. That will be the first name. Then a few days after its birth, the baby is given a second name that has more significance to the family.

In Africa, names sometimes reflect the father's or mother's bloodline, the sex of the child, and its position in the family relative to its brothers and sisters. Special names are given to firstborn, second-born, and third-born; a boy born between two sisters; the last child born; and a baby born with sickness.

Africans attach great importance to naming a child and to the naming celebration.

Through names, a clan has identified its aspirations; it has honored its ancestors, or it has named its current situation, whether it's a good time for the clan or a bad time.

The naming celebration takes place seven or ten days after the baby's birth. Friends and family arrive with gifts.

Men give their gifts for the baby to the father; women give their gifts to the mother. The elder woman or the elder man sprinkles water toward the sky and then whispers the name in the baby's ear. At that point, it is believed that the baby is no longer part of the spirit world, since he or she now has a name. The party lasts several hours, and then as the guests leave, they give their best wishes to the parents, the baby, and the household.

This chapter contains traditional common-use African names with English definitions from four African languages: Swahili, Yoruba, Zulu, and Hausa. For the most part, these names may be proudly given to a boy or a girl, but use the sound of the African word and its meaning in English as your guide to selecting the perfect name for your new baby. Then, in chapter 6, you'll discover hundreds of unique, new names from the same African languages.

SWAHILI

Agreeable:	RADHIYA
Be grateful:	SHUKUMA
Beautiful:	JAMILA
Born at full moon:	BADRU
Born at night:	CHANSIKU
Born during daylight:	NURU
Born during prosperous times, or divine favor:	NEEMA
Born on a cold night:	MBITA
Clean, or pure:	SAFI
Comfort:	FARAJA
Commendable:	HAMIDI
Coral:	MARJANI

Delightful:	MHINA
Destined to rule:	KHALFANI
Dignity, or glory:	JAHA, or JAHI
Distinguished:	SHARUFA
Exalted:	ALI
Faithful:	SADIKI
Fearless person:	JABARI
Firstborn:	MOSI
Flower:	SAHRA
Forceful:	SHOMARI
Forgive, or pardon:	AFU
Fortunate:	MASUD
Gentle:	DALILA
Gift:	HADIYA
God is our salvation:	ISSA
Good:	HASINA
Gorgeous, or precious:	AZIZA
Great lady:	BIMKUBWA
Handsome:	HASANI
Happiness:	RUFANO
Health, or vigor:	AFYA
Intelligent:	ZAKIYA
King:	MWINYI
Lady of the house:	SITI
Life:	AUSHI, or ESHE
Like the moon:	KAMARIA
Lion:	SIMBA
Luck, or fortune:	BAHATI
Master:	MBWANA
Mercy:	REHEMA
Mighty:	JELANI
Noble:	ABUBAKAR

Of noble promise:	BAKARI
Patience rewarded:	SUBIRA
Peace:	SALIIM
Pearl:	LULU
Pledged to live:	KITWANA
Praiseworthy:	AHMED
Predictor of the future:	RAMLA
Princess:	KIBIBI
Righteous:	RASHIDA
Robe of adornment:	JOKHA
Safe:	SALMA
Saintly:	DARWESHI
Savior:	VUAI
Second-born:	PILI
Servant of God:	ABDULLAH
She rises on high:	RUKIYA
Stern:	ABASI
Strong:	ZUBERI
Third-born:	TATU
Trustworthy, or reliable person:	MWAMINI
Victorious:	NASSOR
Wellborn:	ZALIKA
Wonderful:	AJIB
Worshiper of God:	ABDU

YORUBA

Born away from home:	BANDELE
Born during a holiday:	ABEJUNDE
Born during a journey:	ABIONA

Born during winter:	ABEJIDE
Born in honor, or born during the first days of the new year:	ABIOLA
Born on Sunday:	BOSEDE
Born rich, or born to be rich:	ABIMBOLA
Born righteous:	ADIO
Born to be pleasant:	ADUNI
Born to bring joy:	ABAYOMI
Boy has come again:	AKINTUNDE
Brave boy:	AKINS
Child born at the right time:	OMOLARA
Child comes again:	OMOTUNDE
Child who comes and goes:	APARA
Child with curly hair:	DADA
Father comes again:	BABZTUNDE
Father loves us:	BABAFEMI
First child:	AKO
Fulfillment from God:	OLUYEMI
Generous:	ANIMASHANN
God deserves to be praised:	OLUTOSIN
God forgives:	OSAYABA
God gives me joy:	OLUFUNMILAYO
God gives me love:	OLUFUNKE
God has blessed me:	OLUSHOLA
God hears:	OSAHAR
God loves me:	OLUFEMI

God is the victor:	OLUSHEGUN
Good fortune:	FAYOLA
Goodness:	ANIKA
Greatest joy, or highest honor:	OLUBAYO
Happiness, or joy:	AYO
Happiness is eternal:	TITILAYO
Happy one:	OSEYE
He brings royal honor:	ADEAGBO
He came in a joyful time:	ADEBAYO
He fights for what he wants:	AJAMN
Home is filled with honors:	KUNLE
Honor, or wealth, favors me:	OLAFEMI
Honor surrounds me:	OLANIYAN
I am blessed with joy:	AYOBAMI
I am grateful:	MODUPE
In God's hands:	FOLUKE
Joy comes again:	OLATUNDE
Joy enters the house:	AYODELE
Joy is multiplied:	OLABISHI
King:	OBA
King of the world:	OBATAIYE
Like a hero:	AKINWUNMI
Likeness to God:	OKERA
Love:	IFE
Love brings happiness:	IFETAYO
Loved by all:	JUMOKE
Love me:	FEMI
Manly:	ABENA

Morning:	AARO
Mother comes again:	YETUNDE
Much loved:	ADUKE
Noble birth:	ASESIMBA
One born along the road:	ODE
One who has grace:	ENOMWOYI
Peace:	ALAAFIA
Peace on earth:	AIYETORO
Prosperity:	AASIKI
Queen:	TORKWASE
Righteous:	OLODODO
Royal:	ADE
Savior of the people:	OLUGBALA
Second child:	ANO
Sorrow becomes happiness:	EKUNDAYO
Sweetness:	EDE
Thanks to God:	TEMITOPE
There is glory in wealth:	OLANIYI
There is joy:	BAYO
This one will not die:	KOKUMUO
Twin who comes first:	TAIWO
Twin who comes second:	KEHINDE
Wait and enjoy what the world offers:	DUROJAIYE
We asked and got her:	ABEBI
We begged God for it:	AMBE
We gave praises and he came:	AYINDE
We have a boy:	AKINLABI

We have joy:	NAYO
Wealth:	ORO
Worthy of respect:	BADERINWA

ZULU

Adventurer:	ISIHLANHLATHI
Alert, or watchful:	IHLAKAHIPHILE
Balmy breeze:	UMNYELELE
Believer:	OKHOLWAYO
Blessing:	ISIBUSISO
Brother:	UMFOWETHU
Champion:	USHAMPENI
Charm, or give pleasure to:	JABULISA
Companion, or friend:	UMNGANE
Dance with joy:	HAYIYA
Dawn:	NTWELA
Delight:	ETHABISA
Dignity:	ISIKHULU
Do well:	LUNGA
Enchanter:	OTHWEBULAYO
Feather:	ISIHLUPHE
Fighter:	ISILWI
Give honor to, or sing the praises of:	BONGA
Grace, or beauty:	UKUPHIQILIKA
Grandchild:	UMZUKULU
Happiness, or joy:	INJABULO
Honeybee:	INYOSI
I am a man:	NGIYINDODA
I am strong:	NGINAMANDLA

Kindness:	UMUSA
Lady of quality:	ISIKHULUKAZI
Laughter:	INSINI
Let it come:	AYIZE
Love:	THANDA
Man of wisdom:	INGOIBI
Morning star:	INKANGAKUSA
Niece:	UMSHANAKAZI
Obey:	LALELA
Peacemaker:	UMLAMULI
Person in need:	DINGANE
Power, or strength:	AMANDLA
Present, or gift:	ISIPHO
Protector:	ILIHLATHI
Rainfall:	UKUNA
Respect:	ESABA
Reward:	KLOMELA
River:	UMFULA
Ruler, or governor:	INKOSI
Seashell:	INKWINDI
Serenity, or peace:	UKUTHULA
Shower of rain:	ISIHLANJANA
Sing sweetly:	NOWINA
Source of honor:	UDUMO
Source of pleasure:	OKUJABULISAYO
Spring into life:	SWABULUKA
Success:	MPUMELELE
Sunny:	NOMALANGA
Teardrops:	AMACHIPHIZA
Trail of a shooting star:	ULUHUDO
Trusted:	THEMBA
Walk firmly:	BHELEKEQA
Welcome arrival:	HLANGABEZA

HAUSA

Addition to the family:	KARUWA
Appetite for delicacies:	MARMARI
Beautiful, or handsome:	KYAKKYAWA
Become rich:	ARZUTA
Be confident:	HAKIKANCE
Blessing:	ALBARKA
Brave person:	JARUMI
Champion:	ZAKARA
Charm:	FARA'A
Considerate of another's feelings:	KARA
Daughter:	'YA MACE
Dawn:	ASSALATU
Dignity, or respect:	MUTUNCI
Exercise one's power:	BI HAKKI
Exert great effort:	YUNKURA
Faith:	IMANI
Feather:	GASHI
Flight of a bird:	TASHI
Generosity, or generous:	KARIMCI
Gift:	KYAUTA
God's gift:	YOHANCE
Goodness:	KYAU
Harmony:	DAIDAITUWA
Health:	LAFIYA
Hope:	FATA
Important, or valued:	MUHIMMI
Insight:	BASIRA
Intrigue, or fascinate:	KAYATAR
Jewel:	DUTSE

Journey:	TAFIYA
Kind, or kindness:	KIRKI
Lady:	MACE
Laughter, or laugh:	DARIYA
Leader:	SHUGABA
Look around:	WAIGA
Manliness:	MAZAKUTA
Merciful:	TAUSAYI
Mist:	HAZO
My father is exalted:	IBRAHIM
Peace:	LUMANA
Persevere:	NACE
Person of extraordinary ability:	HATSABIBI
Praise:	YABA
Prophet:	ANNABI
Reliable, or trustworthy:	MATABBACI
Rise to power:	KASAITA
Savanna:	DAJI
Shooting star:	MASHI
Sister:	'YAR'UWA
Son:	DA
Steadfast:	TSAYAYYE
Stream:	KORAMA
Strong, or strength:	KARFI
Sweet:	SAKI
Take action:	AIKATA
Truth:	GASKIYA
Wanderer:	GANTALALLE
Warrior:	GWARZO
Wisdom:	HIKIMA

6 ☆ Unique Names from Four African Languages and Their Definitions

Many African-Americans can trace their ancestry to the people who spoke Swahili, Zulu, Hausa, or Yoruba: the people of the Gold Coast, the Ivory Coast, East Africa, and Nigeria. But not everyone knows where their roots originate or the language of their ancestors.

For centuries, African-Americans have been given names acceptable to white society. But take that list of acceptable names and throw it out.

Before you name your child, look at this chapter. In keeping with the American style of independent thinking, this chapter contains hundreds of beautiful, descriptive English words that have been translated into African languages. Although these are not names traditionally used in Africa, they are names your African-American child can wear with pride.

The African words are generally genderless except in their English meaning. They are beautiful on the tongue, they are completely different from most American names, and they have meanings your children will be proud to explain to their friends.

Choosing a name from this list of African words gives your child a name that he or she can hold close and say, "This is my name; it is unlike anyone else's."

Your child will be asked, "What does that name mean?"
The child named Zuberi will be able to reply, "My name
means 'Grow and be strong,' in Swahili." The child named
Zuma will be able to answer proudly, " 'Honey from a
bee' in Hausa."

"My name means 'Faithful' in Yoruba," is what the child
called Olooto will be able to proclaim.

By selecting a name from this list of African words, you
will be saying, "My child, you are an African-American
and I have given you a name I am proud of—a name I
want you to be proud of and live up to."

SWAHILI

Swahili is a Bantu language and part of the Niger-Congo
family of languages. It is spoken in the coastal areas of
East Africa, from southern Somalia to Mozambique, and
in the Congo. Swahili is considered the language of libera-
tion and black power.

Abundance:	MBOBO
Affection, or devotion:	MAHABA
African:	KIAFRIKA
Amber:	KAHARABU
Amulet:	PAGAO
Amuse oneself:	LAABU
Anchor:	NANNGA
Angel:	MALAIKA
Arrive:	SOZA
Arrogant, or proud:	KIBURI
Autumn:	DEMANI
Aviator, or pilot:	MWANACHEWA
Be, or live:	KAA

Be alert:	HAMU
Beat of the heart:	PUMA
Beauty, or charm or grace:	HAIBA
Be curious:	FATIISHA
Be firm in the face of danger:	KITA
Be generous:	KIRIMU
Be glorious:	TAADHIMIKA
Be good; be of use:	FAA
Be happy:	FURAHI
Be honest:	NYOKA
Be industrious, diligent:	BAIBIA
Be just and righteous:	ADILI
Be kind:	TAIBU
Beloved:	HIBIBU
Be lucky:	BAHATIKA
Be on one's guard:	TANADHARI
Be powerful:	JAALI
Be proud:	NYETA
Be quick-witted:	KALAMKA
Be successful:	FANIKIWA
Be thoughtful:	TANDAWAA
Be true:	SADIFU
Be very happy:	LAFUA
Be wealthy:	KWASI
Be well educated:	TABAHANI
Bewitch, or enchant:	ANGA
Be worthy:	STAHIKA
Blessing:	BARAKA
Blood brotherhood:	SOGA
Bloom; be successful:	BARIKI

Boast, or show off:	FAHARI
Bold, or courageous:	JAHINA
Brave, bold, daring person:	CHAGINA
Breath, or essence:	NAFSI
Bright sky:	KWEUPE
Buffalo:	NYATI
Build, or erect:	AKA
Builder:	MJENZI
Bull, or manly:	FAHALI
Butterfly:	NZIGUNZIGU
Call to prayer:	ADHANA
Calm, or quiet:	KIMYA
Capable, or confident:	TASAWARI
Care of the sick:	MAUGUZI
Celebration:	MAADHIMISHO
Character, or quality:	KIUMBO
Charm, or grace:	MATUKO
Charm against lions:	ILIZI
Charming:	MARIDHIA
Chase, or hunt:	SAKA
Cheerful:	CHANGAMFU
Chief, or leader:	AKIDA
Cinnamon tree:	MDALASINI
Clearing up after a rain:	KICHEA
Clever, or open-minded:	ANGAVU
Cloth of gold:	KASABU
Coconut:	KIDAKA
Color:	RANGI
Comfort, or calm:	LIWAZA
Commander:	AMIRI
Companion:	MWANDANI

Companions of Muhammad:	MASAHABA
Comrade:	RAFIKI
Congratulations:	PONGEZI
Consoler:	MFARIJI
Cool season:	KIPUPWE
Copper:	SIFURI
Creation:	HULUKI
Crocodile:	NGWENA
Daintiness:	KIDOMO
Dance:	TAMBA
Dance to rock and roll:	ROKU
Dawn:	CHA
Daybreak, or the dawn:	ALFAJIRI
Daydream:	SINZIA
Delicate:	LAINI
Delightful:	ANISI
Depths of the ocean:	KITITI
Devotion:	HABA
Diamond:	ALMASI
Distant country:	MPOA
Distinguished, or prominent:	KUU
Doll:	MWANASESERE
Do something energetically:	CHARAZA
Dove:	KIPURE
Do very well at something:	META
Dragonfly:	KERENG'ENDE
Dream:	OTA
Early morning:	KUCHA

Echo:	MWANGWI
Eldest son of the house:	KIBWANA
Elegant:	KIMALIDADI
Elephant:	TEMBO
Eloquent person:	MWONGEZI
Enchant:	SIHIRI
Energy, or strength:	KANI
Enjoy oneself:	RAMISI
Enlightened:	ELEKEU
Enterprising person:	MTENDAJI
Esteem, or honor:	KARAMA
Eternal, or without beginning:	AZALI
Excel:	KUKULA
Excellent, or first-class:	BORA
Extravagant:	BADHIRIFU
Family:	MBARI
Farewell:	ALAMSIKI
Fate:	AJALI
Favorite, or pet:	KIPENZI
Fellow countryman:	MKWAO
Femininity:	KIKE
Festival:	KARAMU
Fig tree:	MTINI
Fine rain:	MANYONYOTA
Fire:	MOTO
Fisherman:	MVUVI
Flame:	MEKA
Flower garden:	BUSTANI
Flowering shrub:	MSAMBALE
Foresight, or prudence:	BUSARA
Foretell the future:	SIBU

Forgiveness:	RADHI
Forgiving person:	MSAMEHAJI
Fragrance:	ITURI
Freeman:	MWUNGWANA
Friend, or companion:	MWENZI
Friendliness, or kindness:	MAPENDEZI
Gather for prayer:	TABARUKI
Gazelle, or impala:	KINOKERO
Generous person:	MPAJI
Gentle breeze:	KIPEPO
Glory:	TAADHIMA
Glow:	NAWIRI
Goal:	NIA
Go-getter:	MPASI
Gold:	DHAHABU
Golden oriole:	KIRUMBIZI
Good:	EMA
Good fortune:	GHANIMA
Good luck:	CHUMU
Goodness, or kindness:	LATIFU
Goodwill:	PENDELEO
Grace:	MADAHIRO
Gracious:	MURUA
Grassland, or savannah:	MDAMBI
Grass with blue blossoms:	MFASA
Great, or significant:	ADHIMU
Great depth:	KINA
Great-grandchild:	KITUKUU
Happy person:	MFURAHIVU
Harmony:	ITIFAKI

Harvest:	KIVUNO
Haste, or restlessness:	PAPIO
Health, or vigor:	RAI
Heart, or feeling:	MOYO
Help, or assistance:	MUAWANA
Hero, or warrior:	SHUJAA
Hidden treasure:	KANZI
Hiding place:	OTEO
Holiday:	LIKIZO
Home:	MAKAO
Honest, or upright:	MADHUBUTI
Honey:	ASALI
Honeycomb:	KALALA
Honorable person:	MNYOFU
Honorable reputation:	NEMSI
Hope:	MATARAJIO
Hot season:	CHAKA
Hunter:	MWINDAJI
Imaginative person:	MWAZAJI
Incorruptible person:	MSALIHINA
Inhabitant of the earth:	MLIMWENGU
Innovator:	KIZUSHI
Inquisitive person:	MPEKUZI
Incision made in the ritual of blood brotherhood:	SARE
Intelligence:	AKILI
Intelligent, or clever:	TAMBUZI
In the evening:	JIONI
Inventor:	MZUZI
Iron:	CHUMA
I wish you a long life:	TAHYATI

Jewel:	JOHARI
Jolly person:	MCHEKESHI
Joy:	ANASA
Kindness:	HISANI
Know, or understand:	KOMANYA
Knowledge:	ELIMU
Laugh:	CHEKA
Lead a life of luxury:	TAANASA
Leaf of the coconut palm:	KUTI
Leopard:	CHUI
Life:	MAISHA
Listen carefully:	SIKIO
Live in easy circumstance:	SITAWI
Lordly, or grand:	SEYYEDIA
Love, or fondness:	ASHIKI
Luck, or chance:	JUMU
Magic:	TEGO
Make ready, or prepare:	TAYARISHA
Mango:	EMBE
Manly deeds:	MAUME
Man of good birth:	ADINASSI
Merciful:	RAHIMU
Mercy:	MAJALIWA
Might, or power:	KUDURA
Mint:	NANAA
Miracle:	IBURA
Mirage:	SARABI
Mischievous child:	MTUKUTU
Mist:	KUNGE
Moon:	MWEZI

Moonlight:	MBALAMWEZI
Mountaintop:	NGUU
Muscular:	PIRIKANA
Music:	MUZIKI
Musical instrument:	GUMBU
Necklace:	KIDANI
Nephew or niece:	MPWA
North wind:	KASKAZI
Of good character:	SALIHI
Olive tree:	MZEITUNI
One of twins:	PACHA
One willing to trust others:	MWAMANA
One who can be relied on to give good advice:	MHENGA
One who has power:	MWEZA
One who learns:	MWANACHUO
One who makes things happen:	MWENDELEZI
One who sings:	MTUMBUIZI
Opportunity:	KIKUTI
Origin, or in the old times:	ASILI
Originator:	MUUMBA
Overcast skies:	MAVUNDE
Paradise:	BARAZAHI
Peace:	AMANI
Peacemaker:	MWAMUA
Pelican:	MWALI
Peppermint:	PEREMENDE
Perfume:	MRASHI

Period of changing winds:	TANGAMBILI
Perennial grass:	FEFE
Persevering:	STAHIMILIVU
Person much respected:	KABAILA
Pioneer:	MWANZILISHI
Pious life:	TAWASUFI
Planting time:	KUPANDA
Playful:	PURUPURU
Pleasant person:	MJIBU
Plentiful, or abundant:	NEEMEVU
Plum tree:	MRATABU
Ponder, or meditate:	FIKIRI
Power:	ENZI
Powerful, or strong:	HODARI
Praise:	HAMDU
Prayer, or plea:	DUA
Prayer beads:	TASHIBI
Precious jewel:	KITO
Present, or gift:	ADIA
Pretty girl:	KISURA
Prophet:	RASULI
Propriety, or manners:	JAMALA
Prosperity:	FANAKA
Protect, or defend:	HAMI
Protect by magic:	FINGA
Purify by prayer:	EUA
Purity:	FASEHA
Queen:	KWINI
Quick-witted person:	MWELEWA
Quiet:	RAHA
Radiance:	KIMETA

Range of mountains:	MFULULIZO
Rare, or unobtainable:	ADIMIKA
Reign, or power:	MATAMALAKI
Rejoicing:	KIKORA
Reliable:	AMINIFU
Religion, or faith:	DINI
Respect, or honor:	HADHI
Respected person:	MTUKUFU
Reverence, or worship:	MAABUDU
Revolutionary:	MWANATHAURA
Ride at a gallop:	JOSHI
Ripple, or small wave:	KIWIMBI
River, or lake:	JITO
Roar of waterfalls:	RINDIMA
Rose-apple tree:	MDARABI
Rosebush:	MWARIDI
Ruler, or king:	MFALME
Sailor:	MWANAMAJI
Sand from the seashore:	KIZINGO
Savior:	WPLPZO
Scholar:	MWALIMU
Sea:	BAHARI
Secret:	KISIRI
Secret passage:	PENYENYE
Self-reliance:	KINAYA
Shine, or be bright:	ANGAA
Shining, or twinkling:	MEMETUKO
Shoulder-to-shoulder:	SAMBAMBA
Show kindness:	FADHILI
Sincere friend:	NASHIA
Sister:	DADA
Skillful:	MAHIRI

Sky, or heaven:	MBINGU
Sleep very soundly:	KIGOGO
Small round pumpkin:	KITOMA
Small yellow bird:	CHIGI
Something good:	KINYEMI
Something precious:	DAFINA
Something remarkable:	MWUJIZA
Something sent by God:	MANZILI
Soothsayer:	MWAGUZI
Soul, or spirit:	ROHO
Sound like thunder:	MTUTUMO
Spirit:	PEPO
Spiritual:	KIROHO
Spring tide:	BAMVUA
Stamina, or endurance:	IMARA
Stand up for one's rights:	GOMA
Starling:	KWENZI
Storm:	SHABABU
Stormy sea:	CHACHA
Strength, or power:	BAVU
Strength of character:	MAKINI
Success, or prosperity:	MAFANIKIO
Sugar:	SUKARI
Sun, or sunshine:	JUA
Sun has gone down:	KUMEKUCHWA
Sunrise:	MACHEO
Sunset:	MACHWA
Surf:	MAWIMBI
Swing, or rock:	PEMBEA
Talented:	EREVU
Teach:	ELIMISHA

Teacher, or educator:	MKALIMU
Tell fortunes:	TABIRI
Temptation:	BILISI
Tender, or delicate:	ORORO
Think, or reflect:	DHANI
Think well of oneself:	JINAKI
Thrive, or prosper:	STAKIMU
Tidal wave:	MAUNDIFU
Treasure:	AZIZI
Triumph over something:	SISMANGA
Trusting person:	MSADIKIFU
Truth, or honesty:	KWELI
Try hard:	KUSURU
Twilight:	KISIKUSIKU
Unity:	KIVA
Unyielding:	SHUPAVU
Very small, or tiny:	KATITI
Victor:	NAMBAWANI
Vigor:	TAMBO
Vigorous young man:	BARUBARU
Walk gracefully:	DALJI
Warrior:	ASKARI
Waterbuck:	KURO
Water lily:	MAYUNGIYUNGI
Watershed:	TENGAMAJI
Welcome:	KARIBISHO
Welcome with joy:	SHAGILIA
Well-being:	SALAMA
Well-bred, or gracious:	ADIBU
Well-known, famous:	BAYANA
Well-to-do person:	MDIRIFU

Whirlwind:	CHAMCELA
Whisper:	NONG'ONA
White frost:	SAKITU
Wildcat:	KANU
Wild dove:	HUA
Wilderness:	PORI
Wild lemon tree:	KIDIMU
Wind spirit:	KINYAMKELA
Wisdom:	HEKIMA
Wish:	PENDEKEZO
Work hard:	KAKAMIA
Worshiper:	MWABUDU
Worthy of trust:	AMINI
Writer, or author:	MWANDISHI
Young bird:	FARANGA
Young cock, or rooster:	PORA
Youngest child:	MPENDWA

YORUBA

Yoruba is a Kwa language of the Niger-Congo family. It is spoken in West Africa, Nigeria, Benin, Togo, Dahomey, and also in Brazil and Cuba.

Ability:	AGBARA
Ablaze:	GBINA
Able-bodied:	ALAGBARA
Abundance:	OPO
Action:	ISE
Admirable:	NIYIN
Adornment:	OSO
Adventurer:	ADAWOLE

Affluence:	OPO
Air:	AFEFE
Alive:	YE
Alleluia:	IYIN
Amazement:	IYALENU
Ambitious:	LOKANJUWA
Angel:	ANGELI
Antelope:	ETU
Applause:	IYIN
Arise:	DIDE
Art:	OGBON
Astonishment:	IYALENU
Audacious:	LAIYA
Aware:	FURA
Baptism:	ISAMI
Bashful:	NITIJU
Beautiful:	LEWA
Behave:	HUWA
Believer:	ONIGBAGBO
Beloved:	OLUFE
Benevolent:	RERE
Berry:	ESO
Better:	DARAJU
Bewilder:	DARU
Big:	NLA
Bird:	EIYE
Birth:	IBI
Bless:	BUKUN
Blessing:	IBUKUN
Bloom:	RUWE
Blossom:	TANNA
Blush:	ITIJU

Bold:	LAIYA
Bountiful:	ONINURE
Brave:	LAIYA
Bravery	IGBOIYA
Breeze:	AFEFE
Bright:	GBON
Brilliant:	SAKA
Buck:	OBUKO
Buffalo:	EFON
Builder:	MOLEMOLE
Butterfly:	LABALABA
Calm	RELE
Canary:	EIYE
Capability:	AGBARA
Care:	ANIYAN
Careful:	SORA
Cascade:	OSOORO
Cat:	OLOGBO
Caterpillar:	KOKORO
Ceremonial:	ISIN
Champion:	OGAGUN
Chance:	ALABAPADE
Change:	IPARADA
Chant:	KORIN
Character:	IWA
Charity:	AANU
Charm:	ONDE
Charmer:	AFOGEDE
Cheeky:	LENU
Cheerful:	TUJUKA
Cherish:	SIKE
Chief:	OLOYE

Chill:	OTUTU
Christian:	ONIGBAGBO
Christmas:	KERESIMESI
Chum:	ORE
Church:	SOOSI
Civilization:	OLAJU
Clarion:	FERE
Cleanliness:	IMOTOTO
Clever:	GBON
Cloud:	IKUUKUU
Clout:	INA
Coconut:	AGBON
Cocoon:	EWURUKU
Cognizance:	AMI
Color:	AWO
Colossal:	TOBI
Comfort:	ITUNU
Commendation:	IYIN
Communion:	ISOKAN
Companion:	ENIKEJI
Compassion:	AANU
Compete:	JIJADU
Competitor:	ABANIDU
Complex:	SORO
Compliment:	IDIJU
Comrade:	EGBE
Concern:	ANIYAN
Concord:	ISOKAN
Confident:	DIDAJU
Confront:	DOJUKO
Congratulations:	IYIN
Conquer:	SEGUN

Conqueror:	ASEGUN
Conscientious:	DEEDEE
Consolation:	ITUNU
Contemplate:	RONU
Contribute:	RANLOWO
Control:	AGBARA
Cool, or cold:	TUTU
Cooperation:	IBASEPO
Copper:	BABA
Coral:	IYUN
Cordial:	NIFE
Creation:	EDA
Creator:	ELEDA
Cure:	WOSAN
Curiosity:	IRIDI
Dainty:	DIDUN
Dance:	IJO
Daring:	LAIYA
Dawn:	AFEMOJUMO
Daylight:	OSAN
Dear:	OLUFE
Decency:	TITO
Decisive:	NIPINNU
Declaration:	SISO
Defend:	DABOBO
Deity:	OLORUN
Delicate:	SELEGE
Deliverance:	IGBALA
Demure:	ONITIJU
Different:	YATO
Dignitary:	OLOLA
Dignity:	OLA

Diligence:	APON
Direct:	TAARA
Discovery:	AWARI
Discretion:	OGBON
Distinction:	IYATO
Distinguish:	MO
Doer:	OLUSE
Doll:	OMOLANGI
Dove:	ADABA
Doze:	TOOGBE
Dream:	ALA
Dusk:	SISOKUNKUN
Eager:	NITARA
Eagle:	IDI
Early:	TETE
Earth:	AIYE
Earthquake:	ISELE
East:	GABASI
Eclipse:	ISIJIBO
Education:	EKO
Effort:	IYANJU
Elegant:	DARA
Elf:	IWIN
Elk:	AGBONRIN
Eminence:	GIGA
Enchanter:	OSO
Endeavor:	IYANJU
Endurance:	IROJU
Enigma:	ALO
Enjoy:	GBADUN
Entice:	TAN
Epitome:	IKEKURU

Equality:	DIDOGBA
Essence:	EDA
Eternal:	LAILAI
Evening:	IROLE
Exceed:	REKOJA
Excel:	TAYO
Excitement:	ROGBODIYAN
Existence:	WIWA
Exodus:	IJADE-LO
Expedition:	IYARA
Experience:	AFOJUBA
Extraordinary:	YANILENU
Extravagance:	INAKUNA
Fable:	ITAN
Fair:	LEWA
Fairness:	MIMORA
Fairy:	IWIN
Faith:	IGBAGBO
Faithful:	OLOOTO
Falcon:	ASA
Fame:	OKIKI
Fancy:	IRO
Fantastic:	NIROKURO
Fascinate:	WU
Fate:	ABAFU
Favorite:	AYANFE
Fearless:	LAIFOIYA
Feather:	IYE
Feeling:	IMO
Fellowship:	IDAPO
Female:	ABO
Ferocious:	NIKA

Festival:	AJODUN
Fierce:	RORO
Fine:	DARA
Fire:	INA
Flame:	OLUFE
Flourish:	GBILE
Flower:	ODODO
Forbearance:	IDAWODURO
Foresight:	IMOTELE
Forgive:	DARIJI
Fortify:	DABOBO
Fortunate:	ABAFU
Fountain:	ISUN
Fox:	KOLOKOLO
Friend:	ORE
Frost:	OTUTU
Fulfillment:	IMUSE
Fun:	AWADA
Fundamental:	IDI
Gallant:	LOLA
Gallantry:	IGBOIYA
Garden:	OGBA
Garland:	MARIWO
Gatherer:	ALAKOJO
Genesis:	IBERE
Genius:	OLOYE
Gentle:	NI-IWA
Ghost:	EMI
Giant:	OMIRAN
Gift:	EBUN
Giver:	OLUFUNNI
Glamour:	OOGUN

Glitter:	ITANSAN
Glorify:	YIN-LOGO
Glorious:	LOLA
Glory:	OGO
Goal:	OPIN
Golden:	ONIGOOLU
Goodly:	DIDARA
Gorgeous, or graceful:	DIDARA
Grace:	ANFAANI
Gracious:	OLOORE-OFE
Grand:	TOBI
Grandchild:	OMO-OMO
Gratify:	TELORUN
Gratitude:	OPE
Great:	TOBI
Greeting:	KIKI
Guardian:	OLUTOJU
Guidance:	IFONAHAN
Handsome:	DARA
Harmony:	IREPO
Harp:	HAPU
Hawk:	AWODI
Headstrong:	LAIGBONRAN
Health:	ALAFIA
Heart:	OKAN
Heir:	AROLE
Helper:	OLURANLOWO
Heritage:	OGUN
Hero:	AKONI
History:	ITAN
Holy:	MIMO
Honesty:	OTITO

Honey:	OYIN
Honor:	OLA
Hope:	IRETI
Hug:	FAMORA
Humility:	IRELE
Humor:	EFE
Idea:	IYE
Imagination:	IRO
Imagine:	RO
Important:	PATAKI
Indigo:	ELU
Influence:	AGBARA
Inherit:	JOGUN
Innocence:	AIJEBI
Inquisitive:	WIWADII
Insight:	IMO
Inspiration:	AGBARA
Intelligence:	OYE
Intrigue:	IDITE
Island:	EREKUSU
Ivy:	ITAKUN
Jewel:	OKUTA-IYEBIYE
Jovial:	LAYO
Judgment:	IDAJO
Judicious:	GBON
Justice:	OTITO
Kind:	EGBE
Kitten:	OMO-OLOGBO
Knowing:	GBON
Lady:	OMOGE
Lake:	ADAGUN
Laugh:	RERIIN

Laughter:	ERIN
Law-giver:	OLOFIN
Leader:	ASAAJU
Leaf:	EWE
Learn:	KO-EKO
Legacy:	OGUN
Legendary:	AROSO
Leopard:	EKUN
Liberation, or liberty:	OMNIRA
Light:	IMOLE
Lightning:	MONAMONA
Lion:	KINIUN
Lively:	DARAYA
Loyal:	SOOTO
Luxury:	IGBADUN
Magic:	IDÁN
Magnificent:	TOBI
Man:	OKUNRIN
Mankind:	ARAIYE
Manly:	ABENA
Maturity:	PIPON
Meadow:	PAPA
Merciful:	ALAANU
Mercy:	AANU
Mighty:	LAGBARA
Mint:	EFIRIN
Miraculous:	IYANU
Mistletoe:	AFOMO
Moon:	OSUPA
Myth:	PIPALO
Mythology:	IJARO
Navigator:	ATUKO

Night:	ORU
Ocean:	OKUN
Openhearted:	TUNUKA
Opportunity:	AYE
Overcome:	BORI
Oyster shell:	IPASAN
Palace:	AAFIN
Panther:	AMOTEKUN
Partridge:	APARO
Patience:	SUURU
Peacock:	AGUFON
Perfection:	PIPE
Persevere:	FORITI
Persistence:	IFORITI
Phantom:	IWIN
Philosopher:	OLOGBON
Pioneer:	ASAAJU
Pleasant:	DUN
Pleasing:	WIWU
Plentiful:	OPOLOPO
Plenty:	PUPO
Poet:	AKEWI
Popular:	LOKIKI
Power:	AGBARA
Powerful:	LAGBARA
Praise:	IYIN
Pray:	GBADURA
Prayer:	ADURA
Precious:	IYEBIYE
Pretty:	LEWA
Prevail:	BORI
Pride:	IGBERAGA

Privilege:	ANFAANI
Proclamation:	IKEDE
Profound:	JINLE
Prominence:	YORI
Promise:	ILERI
Protector:	ALAABO
Proud:	GBERAGA
Provide:	PESE
Prowess:	IGBOIYA
Prudence:	OGBON
Pumpkin:	ELEGEDE
Pursue:	LEPA
Quality:	IWA
Radiate:	TAN
Rain:	OJO
Rainbow:	OSUMARE
Ram:	AGBO
Reap:	KORE
Reason:	IDI
Rebel:	OLOTE
Red:	PUPA
Redemption:	IRAPADA
Reflection:	IFIYESI
Refuge:	AABO
Reign:	JOBA
Religion:	ISIN
Renown:	OKIKI
Repent:	RONUPIWADA
Reputation:	OKIKI
Resolve:	PINNU
Respect:	OWO
Revelation:	IFIHAN

Reverence:	IBOWO
Revival:	ISOJI
Reward:	ERE
River:	ODO
Roar:	KE
Romance:	IJARO
Rooster:	AKUKO
Rosary:	TESUBA
Rose:	DIDE
Rugged:	LAITEJU
Runner:	AGANGAN
Sacred:	MIMO
Sacrifice:	EBO
Safe:	LAILEWU
Sage:	OLOGBON
Sailor:	ATUKO
Salvation:	IGBALA
Samaritan:	ALAANU
Satin:	BARANJE
Scholar:	AKEKO
Scrupulous:	NIYE-MEJI
Sculptor:	AFINNA
Sea:	OKUN
Season:	IGBA
Second:	EKEJI
Secret:	NIKOKO
Security:	AABO
Seer:	WOLII
Self-will:	AGIDI
Sensible:	LOYE
Serenity:	IDAKE-RORO
Sermon:	IWAASU

Shadow:	OJIJI
Shell:	EEPO
Shine:	DAN
Shout:	ARIWO
Silent:	DAKE
Silver:	FADAKA
Sincere:	SOOTO
Sing:	KORIN
Sinless:	LAILESE
Sir:	OGBENI
Sister:	ARABINRIN
Skillful:	LOGBON
Sky:	ORUN
Sleepy, or slumber:	TOOGBE
Slender:	TEERE
Smart:	YARA
Smile:	RERIIN
Soft:	DE
Softly:	JEEJEE
Solace:	IRORA
Soldier:	SOJA
Solemn:	NIRONU
Solve:	LADI
Somersault:	TITAKITI
Son:	OMOKUNRIN
Song:	ORIN
Soothe:	PON
Sparkle:	ETA-INA
Sparrow:	OLOGOSE
Spectacular:	AGBIRO
Speed:	IYARA
Spirit:	EMI

Spirited:	YIYARA
Splendid:	DARA
Splendor:	HIHAN
Sprightly:	NI-DIDARAYA
Stamina:	IFORITI
Star:	IRAWO
Start:	BERESI
Sterling:	MO
Storm:	IJI
Storyteller:	AROHIN
Stouthearted:	LAIYA
Strength:	AGBARA
Strive:	BA-JA
Study:	AFIYESI
Stupendous:	NIYANU
Suave:	NIWA
Succeed:	ROPO
Success:	ASEYORI
Sugar:	SUGA
Sun:	OORUN
Sunrise:	OWURO
Sunset:	ASAMALE
Superior:	DARAJU
Surpass:	REKOJA
Surprise:	IYANU
Survive:	PE
Sweet:	DIDUN
Tact:	OGBON
Talker:	OSORO
Teacher:	TISA
Temple:	SOOSI
Tenacious:	RIRO

Tender:	FI-FUN
Tenderness:	IKERA
Terrific:	LEKE
Thinker:	ALASARO
Thoughtful:	LANIYAN
Thunder:	ARA
Tiger:	AMOTEKUN
Tiny:	KERE
To command:	PASE
Today:	LONII
Tornado:	IJI
To seek:	WA KIRI
Tough:	YI
Tranquil:	DIDAKEJE
Tranquility:	IDAKEKEJE
Treasure:	ISURA
Treat:	APEJE
Trinity:	METALOKAN
True:	OTITO
Truehearted:	OLOTITO
Trust:	GBEKELE
Trustworthy:	NITOOTO
Try:	DANWO
Tutor:	OLUKO
Twilight:	AFEEMOJUMO
Twin:	IBEJI
Twinkle:	TAN
Understanding:	IMO
Unite:	SOPO
Universe:	AIYE
Unlimited:	LAINIWON
Unopposed:	LAIDOJUKO

Untainted:	LAISABAWON
Upright:	OLOTITO
Valiant:	LAGBARA
Valuable:	ONIYELORI
Vanquish:	SEGUN
Velvet:	ASO-ARAN
Victorious:	NISEGUN
Vigil:	AISUN
Vigilant:	OLUSORA
Vigor:	AGBARA
Vigorous:	LAIBERU
Vision:	IRAN
Vivacity:	IYE
Vociferous:	ONIGBE
Voracious:	OJEUN
Vow:	EJE
Voyage:	ISIKO
Walk:	RIN
Warrior:	OLOGUN
Wedding:	IGBEYAWO
Welcome:	KAABO
Whirl:	POOYI
Whisper:	SOFOFO
Wholesome:	DARA
Wild:	EHANNA
Wilderness:	AGINJU
Wind:	EFUUFU
Winner:	ASEGUN
Winning:	NIFAIYA
Wisdom:	OGBON
Wizard:	AJE
Woman:	OBINRIN

Wonder:	IYANU
World:	AIYE
Worshiper:	OLUSIN
Worthy:	NIYELORI
Writer:	AKOWE
Yearning:	IYONU
Young:	SOMODE
Zeal:	ITARA
Zenith:	OTE

ZULU

Zulu is a Bantu language, part of the Niger-Congo family of languages. It is spoken in southeast Africa.

Acumen:	UBUQILI
Admire:	BABAZA
Adonis:	ISOKA
Adore:	THANDISISA
Alive:	USEKHONA
All hail:	HALALA
Aloe:	UMHLABA
Alone:	PHANQUZA
Amazement:	UKUMANGALA
Ambassador:	ISIGIJIMI
Amen:	AMENI
Amuse:	DLALISA
Ancestor:	UGOGO
Antelope:	INYAMAZANE
Appear:	BONAKALA
Appreciation:	UKUTHUTHUKA
Apricot:	ILIBHILIKOSA

Astonish:	MANGALISA
Attractiveness:	UBUWOZAWOZA
Autumn:	UKWINDLA
Azure:	ILIFEFE
Babe:	INGANE
Bantu peoples:	UMUNTU
Beauty:	UBUHLE
Behold:	BONA
Be profitable:	SIZA
Be sharp:	SIKA
Bird:	INYONI
Birth, or beginning:	UKUQALA
Blind, or dazzle:	PHANDLA
Blossom:	IMBALI
Boldness, or daring:	NGESIBINDI
Boy, or male child:	UMFANA
Bravery:	UBUQHAWE
Brawn:	IZIGALO
Breadwinner:	ULUZIME
Bring forth:	VEZA
Bring together:	BUTHA
Brotherhood:	UBUZALWANE
Buck:	BHEKUZA
Builder:	UMAKHI
Butterfly:	ULUVEMVANE
Canary:	ILIKHANELI
Carefulness:	ISANDLA
Carriage, or bearing:	ISIMO
Charmer:	UMTHONYI
Clever person:	INGEWEPHESHI
Cloudburst:	UMVIMBI
Cobra:	IMFEZI

Cocksure:	NEQINISO
Come together:	QOQANA
Come to life:	VELA
Comfort:	INDUDUZO
Commander:	UMPHATHI
Compassion:	UBUBELE
Contemplate:	CEBA
Crack of thunder:	UKUKLAKLABULA
Cry of a bird:	UKUKHALA
Daring:	ISIBINDI
Daughter:	INDODAKAZI
Dazzle:	PHANDLA
Defend:	FUKAMELA
Defender:	UMPHIKELI
Defiance:	INJAKA
Determination:	IBHEJI
Doll:	UNDOLI
Do one's best:	CEBENGELA
Drive, or force forward:	QHUBA
Driving wind:	ISIPHEPHO
Drop of water:	ILICONSI
Duty:	IMFANELO
Eagle:	UKHOZI
Earth:	UMHLABATHI
Earthquake:	UKUDIKIZA
Ebony:	UHLOBO LOMUTHI
Eminence:	IKUPHAKAMA
Enjoy:	JABULELA
Extraordinary thing:	ISIMANGALISO
Faith:	ILITHEMBA
Fancy:	CABANGA
Fate:	ISINQUMELO

Fawn:	CEBEDISA
Fellow:	UMUFO
Fellowship:	UKUHLANGANA
Firstborn:	UTSHANA
Flame:	VUTHA
Flower:	QHAKAZA
Fondness:	ISISA
Force, or strength:	INDLUZULA
Fragrance:	AMAKHA
Free will:	UMPHIMBO
Frolic:	TSHEKULA
Galaxy:	UMTHALA
Gem:	IYIGUGU
Gentleman:	INJITIMANE
Gentle wind:	UMNYELELA
Give one's word:	THEMBISA
Give shelter to:	BHACISA
Glory, or splendor:	INKAZIMULO
Good judgment:	UMQONDO
Goodness:	UBUHLE
Good omen:	UMBONANHLE
Great kindness:	ISISA
Greatness:	UBUKHULU
Grow well:	VUMA
Grow wise:	HLAKANIPHA
Handsome:	ILIGEZA
Have the upper hand:	PHATHA
Headdress of feathers:	ISILUBA
Healthiness:	UKUHILA
Herald:	UMANDULELI
Hero:	IMBUDLE
Hold in the arms:	SINGATHA

Hold one's own:	ZABALAZA
Home:	ILIKHAYA
Honesty:	UBUGOTHO
Honor, or respect:	ISIQHOLISO
Hope:	ETHEMBA
Hope for success:	UKUTHEMBISA
Humility:	INTOBEKO
Independence:	UKUZIMELA
Inheritance:	ILIFA
In silence:	NQOKUTHULA
Interesting:	OKUNAKISAYO
In the open air:	NGAPHANDLE
Jewel, or treasured object:	ILIGUGU
Judgment:	INGQONDO
Keep good health:	PHILA KAHLE
Kingdom:	UMBUSO
Kiss:	ANGA
Lady:	INKOSIKAZI
Lark:	ILINQOMFI
Leader:	UMHOLI
Leaf:	ILIKHASI
Leopard:	ILIJELE
Life:	UKUZWA
Lightning:	UMBANI
Lily:	UMDUZE
Lion:	INGONYAMA
Live:	ZWA
Lively, or merry:	LIXUBUNGU
Look up to, or respect:	HLONIPHA
Lovable:	BHEKA
Lovingly:	NGOTHANDO

Loyalty:	UKUTHEMBEKA
Luck:	INHIANHLA
Magic:	UMLINGO
Make, or produce, or create:	ENZA
Make a stand:	VIMBELEZA
Make one's way:	HAMBA
Make peace:	LAMULA
Make waves:	KAPAZA
Male:	ISILISA
Martyr:	UMFELUKHOLO
Master, in command:	INDUNA
Meet one's fate:	ENZAKALA
Mercy:	UBUBELE
Miracle:	ISIMANGALISO
Mischief:	UKONA
Mist:	INKUNGU
Mockingbird:	ISANZWILI
Modesty:	IZINHLONI
Moon:	INYANGA
Morning:	ILISASA
Music:	UMNYUZIKI
Mystify:	SITHIBEZA
Name, or reputation:	ULUDUMO
Nation:	ISIZWE
Nature, or life force:	UNOMUNTU
Newcomer:	ISIFIKI
Night:	UBUSUKU
Nightfall:	UKUHWALALA
Nobility:	UBUNTU
Novelty:	UBUSHA
Oak:	ILIOKI

Obedience:	UKULALELA
Occasion, or special event:	UMKHOSI
Occurrence of awe-inspiring proportion:	UMHLOLA
Ocean:	ULWANDLE
Open country:	UDALALA
Opportunity:	ILITHUBA
Opulence:	UBUCWICWICWI
Organizer:	UMHLELI
Originator:	UMQAMBI
Ours:	ABETHU
Outburst of excitement:	ILIDLINGOZI
Outdo:	EQA
Outwit:	GANYA
Overwhelm:	AHLULA
Owl:	ISIKHOVA
Ox:	INKABI
Pacify:	THULISA
Pal:	UNTANGA
Palace:	ILIPHALASI
Palm tree:	ILILALA
Panther:	ILIHLOSI
Parade:	UKUBUKISA
Paradise:	ILIPHARADISI
Par excellence:	KAKHULU
Parrot:	UPHOLI
Partridge:	ILITHENDELE
Party:	ILIPHATHI
Passion:	SHELA
Passionately:	KAKHULU
Patience:	UKUBEKEZELA

Patriarch:	INZALAMIZI
Patter of rain:	QAPHAZA
Pay tribute:	ETHULA
Peacock:	ILIPIGOGO
Pearl:	ILIPHERA
Pedestal:	INCWELANA
Pelican:	ILIFUBA
Perceive:	ZWA
Perception:	UKUZWA
Perfection:	UBUHLE DU
Performer:	OWENZAYO
Perfume, or fragrance:	USENDE
Perseverance:	UKUQINISELA
Persevere:	KHUTHAZELA
Persistence:	ULUNEMBE
Personality:	ISITHUNZI
Persuasion:	INTAMBISO
Pick of the bunch:	ULUKLOKO
Pile of clouds:	FUTHUZELA
Pilot:	UMKHAPHI
Pioneer:	UMCABI
Place confidence in or reliance on:	GABA
Place of refuge:	INQABA
Planter of crops:	UMTSHALI
Play or frolic:	DLALA
Pleasantly:	KAMNANDI
Plenty:	OKUNINGI
Plum:	ILIPULAMU
Plume:	ILIGUBHELA
Poem:	INKONDLO
Politeness:	ISIZOTHA

Pomegranate:	ILIHALANANDA
Pomp:	UBUKHOSI
Pool of water:	ISICHIBI
Positively:	NGEMPELA
Power of thought:	INHLIZIYO
Power, or ability:	ISIVAMELO
Power, or control:	UBUKHOSI
Praise:	BABAZA
Prayer:	UMKHULEKI
Preacher:	UMSHUMAYEI
Prediction:	OKUBIKWE
Preserve:	LONDOLOZA
Prestige:	UBUNZIMA
Prettiness:	UBUBLE
Pride:	UKUZIDLA
Privilege:	ILILUNGELO
Prize:	UMVUZO
Produce:	ENZA
Producer:	UMENZI
Prominence:	UKUQHAMA
Propriety:	IMFANELO
Prosperity:	UKUCHUMA
Protect:	LONDA
Provide:	NIKA
Prowess:	ISIBINDI
Pumpkin:	ILITHANGA
Pureness:	UBUMHLOPHE
Purify:	GEZA
Purple:	UBUNSOMI
Purr:	NDONDA
Pursue relentlessly:	KHONSA
Put confidence in:	GABA

Put spirit into:	CIJA
Quality person:	ILIKHWALITHI
Queen:	UKHWINI
Radiate:	ENABA
Radical:	ISIQU
Rain:	IMVULA
Raise hopes:	ETHEMBISA
Ram:	INQAMA
Rascal:	ILISHINGA
Raven:	HULAZA
Reader:	OFUNDAYO
Realize, or accomplish:	ENZA
Reap:	VUNA
Reason, or intellect:	INGQONDO
Reassure:	ETHEMBISA
Rebel:	HLUBUKA
Rebuild:	VUSELELA
Recognition:	UKUQABUKA
Redeemer:	UMAPHULI
Redemption:	INSINDISO
Relax:	VOVOVONISA
Rely on:	ETHEMBA
Renew, or reinvigorate:	VUSA
Rescuer:	UMSINDISI
Revelry:	UKUZITIKA
Reverence:	INHLONIPHO
Riches:	INGLEBO
Righteousness:	ISIQONDO
Rise:	PHUMA
Rise to power:	DLONDLOBALA
River crossing:	IZIBUKO
Roar like a lion:	BHODLA

Rose:	ILIROZA
Royalty:	ILIKOMKHULU
Run lightly:	QANANAZA
Run wild:	HLANTULA
Runner:	ISIGIJIMI
Rush of wind:	ISIVUNGUZANE
Rustle:	HASHAZA
Sacrifice:	UMNIKELO
Safety:	UKULONDEKA
Sailor:	ILITILOSI
Salute, or greet:	BINGELELA
Salvation:	UKUSINDISA
Satisfy:	ANELISA
Savior:	UMSINDISI
Say farewell:	VALELISA
Say one's prayers:	THANDAZA
Scholarship, or learning:	ULWAZI
Scientist:	UMSAYENSI
Sea:	ULWANDLE
Sea breeze:	UMNYELELE
Search:	FUNA
Security:	UKULONDEKA
Seek:	QAZA
Self-confidence:	UMHLWENGA
Self-control:	UMNYAMEZELE
Self-esteem:	UKUZAZI
Self-respect:	UKUZIHLONIPHA
Self-seeker:	OZIFUNELAYO
Self-will:	INKANI
Sense of prestige:	ULUHLONZI
Set free:	KHULULA
Set right:	LUNGISA

Shine:	KHANYA
Show delight:	ENANELA
Show favor:	BANDLULULA
Show off:	BHENSA
Shy:	PHONSA
Sigh of wind:	BUBULA
Silk:	USILIKA
Sing:	CULA
Sing as a bird:	KHALA
Sing softly:	ZIKA
Sister:	UDADE
Sky:	ILIZULU
Smart:	SHISA
Smooth over:	TOBISA
Soar:	ZULA
Softly:	KANCANE
Soft sound:	UMSINJWANA
Son:	INDODANA
Song:	ILIGAMA
Soul:	UMOYA
Sparrow:	UNDLUNKULU
Speak authoritatively:	KHULUMA
Speak out:	PHUMSESELA
Spirit:	UMOYA
Spirited young man:	ILIBHABHA
Spirit of life:	UMOYA
Spiritual brother:	UMZALWANA
Splash with color:	PHUKUTHISA
Split one's sides with laughing:	YIYITHEKA
Spoil a child:	BONGOZA
Sport, or play:	UMDLALO

Sportsman:	UMDLALI
Spot of rain:	KHIFIZA
Spread the wings:	PHAPHALAZA
Spring:	INTWASAHLOBO
Sprinkle:	FAFAZA
Sprint:	JUBALALA
Spunk:	ISIBINDI
Squirrel:	INGWEJEJE
Stand firm:	GXILA
Stand out:	QHAMA
Stealth:	ISINYELELA
Sterling:	ILISTELINGI
Streak of luck:	INHLANHLANA
Stream of water:	UMFDLANA
Strive:	ZAMA
Strong character:	UBUQOTHO
Strong man:	ILIBHELEBA
Struggle to get free:	SHUKUZA
Strut:	CONDOZA
Study:	UKUFUNDA
Style:	INDLELA
Succeed, or prosper:	PHUMELELA
Sugar:	USHUKELA
Sun, or sunshine:	ILILANGA
Sunny person:	ISIJABULI
Superman:	ISIQHWAGA
Surface of the water:	ULUKHUMBI
Surpass:	DLULA
Survivor:	OWASINDAYO
Sustain, or prove:	QUINISA
Swagger:	KHUNSELA
Swashbuckler:	ILIQHOLOSHA

Sweetheart:	ISINGANE
Swift runner:	INGIJIMI
Swimmer:	OHLAMBAYO
Sympathy:	ULUZWELA
Tadpole:	INGCLUNGULU
Talent:	ISIPHIWO
Tall grass:	ISIKHOTHA
Take care:	QAPHELA
Take notice:	NAKA
Take refuge:	BALEKELA
Temper, or vivacity:	IMPEKUMPEKU
Thanksgiving:	OKOKUBONGA
Thrive:	KHULA
Thunder:	DUMA
Tiger:	ILITHAYIGA
To charm:	HAWULA
Tolerate:	VUMELA
To reason:	ZINDLA
Travel:	HAMBA
Treasure:	ILIGUGU
Treat kindly:	WOTHA
Truth:	ILIQINISO
Tulip:	INCEMBE
Turtledove:	ILIHOBHE
Twinkling:	UKUPHAZIMA
Understanding:	UKUQONDA
United States:	IMELIKA
Unity:	UBUNYE
Uplift:	FUKULA
Valor:	UBUQHAWE
Victory:	UKWAHLULA
Vigor:	AMANDLA

Virility:	UBUDODA
Vivacity:	UKUQINA
Voyage:	ULUHAMBO
Walk over:	ALUSA
Walk softly:	CATHAMA
Waterfall:	IMPOPHOMA
Water lily:	ILIZIBU
Wealth:	UMNOTHO
Wilderness:	INDLE
Willow:	UMNYEZANE
Willpower:	INHLIZIYO
Win:	AHLULA
Wind:	UMOYA
Winding path:	ILIGWINCI
Windstorm:	ISIPHEPHO
Work hard:	SHIKASHIKEKA
Young tree:	ILIKLUME
Youthfulness:	UBUSHA
Zenith:	UMPHEZULU
Zest:	INKUTHALO

HAUSA

Hausa is an Afro-Asiatic language. It is spoken in northern Nigeria and southern Niger.

Ability:	IYAWA
Abundance:	YAWA
Accomplish:	CIMMA
Achieve:	SAMU
Active, or energetic:	KUZARI
Admiration, or admire:	SHA'AWA

Advance, or progress, or move forward:	CI-GABA
Advice:	SHAWARA
Air:	ISKA
Alive:	A RAYE
Allegiance:	BIYAYYA
Alone:	KADAI
Amount to:	KAI
Amuse:	BA
Ancestry:	JINI
Angel:	MALA'IKA
Antelope:	MAZO
Apple:	TUFFA
Artistic:	FASAHA
Be alert:	FADAKAR
Bee:	ZUMA
Bell:	KARARRAWA
Be ready:	SHIRYA
Bible:	LINJILA
Big, or large:	BABBA
Bird:	TSUNTSU
Birth:	HAIHUWA
Blossom:	FURE
Blow of a slight breeze:	KADA
Brain:	KWANYA
Bravery:	JARUNTAKA
Breath:	NUMFASHI
Brilliant:	HAZAKA
Brother:	DAN'UWA
Brotherhood:	DARIKA
Buffalo:	BAUNA
Businessman of prominence:	ATTAJIRI

Calm:	NITSUWA
Camaraderie:	KAWANCE
Can do:	IYA
Cane of bamboo:	GORA
Careful, or cautious:	HANKALI
Cassia tree:	RUNHU
Cat:	KYANWA
Celebration, or ceremony:	BIKI
Character:	HALI
Charitable person:	KARIMI
Charity:	SADAKA
Cinnamon:	KIRFA
Clap of thunder:	ARADU
Clever:	AZANCI
Cold season:	HUNTURU
Colt:	DUKUSHI
Command, or order:	UMARNI
Commander:	KWAMANDA
Companion:	ABOKI
Competition, or contest:	GASA
Comrade:	ABOKI
Congratulations:	MURNA
Congregation:	MASALLATA
Consider others' advice:	JINJINA
Constant:	KULLUM
Control, or power:	IKO
Copper:	TAGULLA
Coral:	MURJANI
Corona of the sun:	SANSANI
Country:	KASA
Countryside:	KARKARA

Courage:	JARUNTAKA
Courteous:	LADABI
Court of the chief:	FADA
Cousin:	DAN'UWA
Creation, or create:	HALITTA
Crest of a bird:	ZANKO
Crocodile:	KADA
Cross a river:	KETARE
Crown:	KAMBI
Crusade:	JIHADI
Cunning:	WAYO
Dance:	RAWA
Dare, or challenge:	KALUBALANTA
Darkening of the sky:	RINE
Daydream:	MARARKI
Decency:	NAGARTA
Decision:	HUKUNCI
Defend:	TSARE
Defiance:	KANGARA
Delight:	MURNA
Deliverance:	CETO
Depend on:	DOGARA
Destiny, or fate:	KADDARA
Diamond:	LU'ULU'U
Different:	DABAM
Diligent:	HIMMA
Doctor:	LIKITA
Dream:	MAFARKI
Dry season:	RANI
Duty:	AIKI
Eagle:	GAGGAFA
Earth, or the planet:	DUNIYA

Ebony:	KANYA
Echo:	AMSA
Ecstasy:	SHAUKI
Elephant:	GIWA
Embrace:	RUNGUMA
Eminent:	MASHAHURI
Empire:	DAULA
Endurance:	DAUREWA
Energetic:	MUZAKKARI
Energy:	KUZARI
Enthusiasm:	SHA'AWA
Equal:	DAIDAI
Equality:	DAIDAITO
Esteem:	DARAJA
Eternity:	DAWWAMA
Evening:	MARAICE
Excel:	FIFITA
Excitement:	ZUMUDI
Existence, or life:	RAYUWA
Expert:	GWANI
Expertise:	GWANINTA
Extravagant:	ALMUBAZZARI
Fable:	HIKAYA
Fairness, or fair:	ADALCI
Fame:	SUNA
Family:	IYAYE
Famous:	MASHAHURI
Fantasy:	TATSUNIYA
Fate:	KADDARA
Feel, or touch:	TABA
Fellow:	TALIKI
Feminine:	TAMATA

Festival:	BIKI
Fig:	CEDIYA
Fire:	WUTA
First:	FARKO
First-rate:	NAGARTA
Flare up of fire:	KUFULA
Fleecy white cloud:	GAJIMARE
Flower:	FURE
Flower garden:	GADINA
Folktale:	TATSUNIYA
Force of personality:	KWARJINI
Foresight, or insight:	TSINKAYA
Forgiveness:	GARARA
Formidable:	GAGARUMI
Forward:	GABA
Foundation, or source:	TUSHE
Fox:	YANYAWA
Fragrance:	KANSHI
Free:	'YANTACCE
Freedom:	'YANCI
Fresh, or new:	SABO
Friendship:	ABOTA
Fun:	NISHADI
Future:	GABA
Gain, or profit:	RIBA
Gazelle:	BAREWA
Glorify:	GIRAMA
Glory, or honor:	SUNA
Grass:	CIYAWA
Handshake:	MUSAFAHA
Harvest season:	KAKA
Hawk:	SHAHO

Headman:	HELUMA
Heal:	WARKE
Healer:	BOKA
Heart:	ZUCIYA
Hearth:	MURFU
Heaven:	SAMA
Height, or peak:	GANIYA
Heir:	MAGAJI
Holy, or holiness:	TSARKI
Home:	GIDA
Homeland:	KASA
Honesty:	GASKIYA
Honey:	ZUMA
Honor, or dignity:	MUTUNCI
Hornet:	RINA
Hot season:	BAZARA
Hug, or embrace:	RUNGUMA
Idea, or plan:	SHIRI
Ignite:	KUNA
Illuminate:	HASKAKA
Improve, or make better:	GYARA
Indigo:	BABA
Inflame:	ZUGA
Influence:	KASASHEN
Ingenious:	FASAHA
Inherit:	GADA
Insistent:	NACI
Intuition:	ILHAMI
Island:	TSIBIRI
Join, or bring together:	HADA
Joke:	WASA

Joy:	MURNA
Judgment:	HAKUNCI
Just, or fairness:	ADALCI
Justice:	SHARI'A
Kinsman:	DAN'UWA
Kiss:	SUMBATA
Know:	SANI
Knowledge:	ILIMI
Lace:	LESHI
Lark:	TSIGI
Lead, or direct:	SHUGABANTA
Leaf of a tree:	GANYE
Learn:	KARU
Leaves fall:	ZUBA
Leopard:	DAMISA
Liberty:	'YANCI
Life:	RAI
Light, or brightness:	HASKE
Light a fire:	KUNNA
Lightning:	ARADU
Lily:	BADO
Lion:	ZAKI
Literature:	
Live:	ZAUNA
Logic, or sense:	HANKALI
Love:	KAUNATA
Lovebird:	KALO
Loyalty:	BIYAYYA
Luck:	SA'A
Luxury:	ALATU
Maiden:	BUDURWA
Majesty:	ALFARMA

Male, or masculine:	NAMIJI
Man:	MUTUM
Manners:	LADABI
Merriment:	ANNASHCIWA
Messiah:	ALMASIHU
Mistletoe:	KAUCI
Modern:	ZAMANI
Modest:	KUNYA
Monarchy:	MULUKIYA
Moon:	WATA
Morning:	SAFIYA
Muscular:	MURDEDE
Music:	KIDA
Nation:	AL'UMMA
New:	SABO
Night:	DARE
Nobility:	SARAKAI
Oasis:	ZANGO
Objective, or goal:	MAKASUDI
Ocean:	TEKU
Orchard:	GARKA
Origin, or ancestry:	ASALI
Outside, or outdoors:	WAJE
Palace:	FADA
Papaya tree:	GWANDA
Parade:	FARETI
Paradise:	ALJANNA
Parrot:	AKU
Peacock:	DAWISU
Peak:	GANIYA
Pelican:	KWASAKWASA
Perceive:	JI

Perceptive:	FAHIMI
Physician:	LIKITA
Pineapple:	ABARBA
Plum:	DINYA
Poem, or poetry:	WAKA
Poet:	MAWAKI
Polite:	LADABI
Possible:	YIWUWA
Practical:	AMFANI
Prayer:	SALLA
Precious:	DARAJA
Prestigious:	KWARJINI
Prince:	YARIMA
Princess:	GIMBIYA
Privilege:	GATANCI
Produce, or make:	YI
Progress:	CI-GABA
Proper, or correct:	DAIDAI
Proud:	ALFAHARI
Prudence:	HANKALI
Pumpkin:	KABEWA
Purity:	TSARKI
Purple, or plumlike:	ALGASHI
Pursue:	FAFARA
Quality:	AMINCI
Queen:	SARAUNIYA
Quest:	BIDA
Quiet:	SHIRU
Rain:	RUWA
Rainy season:	DAMINA
Ram:	RAGO
Rare, or one of a kind:	NADIRI

Reality:	HAKIKA
Reap, or harvest:	GIRBA
Reason:	HANKALI
Red:	JA
Reed:	IWA
Religion:	ADDINI
Remedy:	MAGANI
Renew:	SABUNTA
Renown:	SHAHARA
Reputation, or honor:	IRILI
Reward:	LADA
Rhythm:	KARI
Rich, or wealthy:	ARZIKI
Riches:	DUKIYA
River:	KOGI
Roar of a fire:	RURA
Rooster:	ZAKARA
Royalty, or royal:	SARAUTA
Sacred:	TSARKI
Saint:	WALI
Salute:	JINJINA
Savior:	MACECI
Scarlet:	JAWA
Sea:	TEKU
Secrecy:	ASIRI
Seek:	NEMA
Sensible:	HANKALI
Serious:	TSANANI
Sermon:	WA'AZI
Shadow, or shade of a tree:	INUWA
Share:	RABA

Sharp, or keen:	KAIFI
Shelter:	MAFAKA
Shield:	GARKUWA
Shine:	HASKA
Shrewd:	WAYO
Sibling:	DAN'UWA
Siesta:	KAILULA
Silent, or silence:	SHIRU
Silver:	AZURFA
Singer:	MAWAKI
Skill, or ability:	IYAWA
Sky:	SAMA
Smart:	KWALWA
Smooth:	SUMUL
Snake charmer:	GARDI
Snow:	KANKARA
Soft:	TAUSHI
Soldier:	SOJA
Somersault:	ALKAHURA
Song:	WAKA
Sparrow:	GWARA
Spin round and round:	JUYA
Spirit:	KURWA
Splash:	FANTSAMA
Sprinkle:	YAYYAFA
Squeeze:	MATSA
Stallion:	INGARMA
Stamina:	KUZARI
Star in the heavens:	TAURARUWA
Stature:	GIRMA
Storm clouds:	HADARI
Strive:	DAGE

Struggle:	FAMA
Study, or learn:	KOYA
Sturdy:	GWABI
Style:	HAZBIYA
Success, or victory:	NASARA
Successful:	KAMMALA
Sugar:	SUKARI
Sun:	RANA
Superior:	MAFIFICI
Survive:	RAYU
Tender:	TANDA
Thoughts, or feelings:	RAI
Thrill:	BURGE
Thunder:	TSAWA
Traveler:	MATAFIYI
Treasure:	DUKIYA
Tropical forest:	KURMI
Trust:	AMINCEWA
Trustworthy:	AMINTACCE
Twilight:	MAGARIBA
Upright, or just:	NAGARI
Valor:	JARUNTAKA
Valuable, or important:	DARAJA
Velvet:	KARAMMISKI
Victory:	NASARA
Vitality:	KUZARI
Water lily:	BADO
Well-bred:	LADABI
Well-to-do:	SAMU
Whirlwind:	GUGUWA
Wind:	ISKA
Wit, or humor:	BARKWANCI

World:	DUNIYA
Worldly:	BADUNIYE
Worthy:	DARAJA
Writer:	MARUBUCI
Youthfulness:	YARANTAKA
Zeal:	KWAZO
Zenith:	GANIYA

✦ *Pronunciation Guide*

African languages are written according to what the ear hears. Words are usually spelled phonetically and are fairly easy to pronounce.

Although I am not an African linguistics expert, I can provide these simple, basic guidelines.

Pronounce each syllable. In English, words are often cut short and we slide on the syllables. But in Swahili, Yoruba, Zulu, and Hausa, you must pronounce each syllable without sliding into the next syllable.

Pronounce each vowel fully: Without adding any sound to the front or the back of the vowel, pronounce *a, e, i, o,* and *u* with individual clarity. Pronounce each vowel you see in a word as if the vowel stands alone. If there are two vowels together, pronounce each one.

SWAHILI

Swahili uses the same vowels as English: *a, e, i, o,* and *u.* But the pronunciation of the vowels is a bit different. In English, we often slide on the end of a vowel by closing our mouth at the end of it. In Swahili, you almost want to cut off the sound of the vowel before you end it, as if each vowel were a separate syllable.

A is pronounced like the *a* in *father* or *far*.

E is pronounced like the *a* in *May*.

I is pronounced like the *e* in *me*.

O is pronounced like the *o* in *globe*.

U is pronounced like the *u* in *rude*; if *u* is at the beginning of a word, do not put a *y* sound in front of it as we do in the English pronunciation of the letter *u*; begin the word with the sound of *oo* as in the word *to*.

Vowel sounds are always pure, like the sounds in the words above. Even when a vowel is stressed, it is pronounced as if you were saying the vowel by itself without sliding into the letter next to it. For instance, when you see *ei*, pronounce both the *e* and the *i*; the sound will be like the English word *say*. When you see *ai*, the sound will be like the English word *cry*. When you see *au* together, the sound will be like the English word *how*.

Swahili consonants are the same as English consonants, with the exception of the letters *c, q,* and *x*. *C* is replaced by *s* or *k, q* is replaced by *k* or *kw*, and *x* is replaced by *ks*.

F always sounds like the *f* in *famous*, never like the *f* in *of*.

G always sounds like the *g* in *go*, never a soft *g* as in *George*.

S always sounds like the *s* in *Swahili*. When *s* is a *z* sound, it is spelled with a *z*.

Ch is pronounced just as you would in English, like the word *church*.

Sh is pronounced like the English *sh*, as in the word *shine*.

Th is pronounced like the sound in *think*.

Dh is pronounced like the *th* in the English word *that*.

R is rolled, almost like a Spanish *r*.

Kh is pronounced in the back of the throat; it's a rough sound, like the word *challah*.

Gh is also pronounced in the back of the throat—a gutteral sound—but many nonnative Swahili speakers use a *g* for the *gh* sound.

M at the beginning of a word is always spoken as its own syllable. Do not slide the *m* into the next syllable; pronounce the *m*, then pronounce the vowel or consonant that follows.

N is pronounced like the English-language *n*, but note that when *n* is followed in Swahili by a vowel, it is written as *ny*. It is not spoken as its own syllable but is combined with the vowel sound, like the Russian word *nyet*, or the Spanish word *señor*.

Ng sounds like the *ng* in the English word *ringer*. There is no hard *g* sound in its pronunciation.

YORUBA

A general difference between the vowel sounds of Yoruba and those of English is that the Yoruba vowels are unglided, meaning there is no change in the quality of the vowel as it is being pronounced. For instance, when pronouncing the English vowel *o* in *go*, there is a change in the sound of the vowel at the end. But in Yoruba, the *o* is a pure, very short sound with no change in the sound at the end.

Yoruba has seven vowels:

i as in *eat*

e as in *fate*

eh as in *set*

a as in *not*

ah as in *loss*

o as in *soak*

u as in *toot*

in as in *pinch*

en as in *bench*

an, as in *launch*

un as in *June*

Yoruba consonants are pronounced as follows:

b, *d*, *g*, *t*, *k*, *m*, *n*, and *f* are the same as in English; *w* and *y* sound the same as in English except that when they are in front of a nasal vowel, they are also nasalized, as in the English word *way*;

j as in *joe*

h as in *hoe*

s as in *see*, a whistling sound

sh as in *she*

m and *n* usually sounded nasally, as *ng* in the word *song*

r as in the Spanish word *pero*

gb as a single sound, the *g* sound made in the back of the throat and the *b* sound made with the lips but almost kept inside the mouth

kw pronounced as *k*

kp pronounced as a single sound, as in the word *puff*

ch as in *church*

gw as *g*

ng as in *sing*

nw as a single sound: *n*

ny as in the French word *agneau*.

ZULU

Pronounce each syllable individually rather than sliding from one syllable to the next. Zulu has implosive and explosive sounds. The implosive sound is written and sounds like the English letter *b*, as in the word *back*. The explosive sound is written and sounds like the English combination *bh*, as in the word *barber*.

Zulu vowels are similar to English vowels: *a, e, i, o,* and *u*.

A is pronounced like the *a* in *bar*.

E is pronounced like the *e* in *pen*.

I is pronounced like the *i* in *pity*.

O is pronounced like the *o* in *location*.

U is pronounced like the *oo* in *foot*.

Consonants in Zulu are the same as they are in English, with some exceptions:

J is pronounced like the *dg* sound in the word *judge*.

G is a hard *g*, as in the word *go*.

J is pronounced as *y*, as in the word *yet*.

Kh is pronounced as a hard *k*, as in the word *king*.

M is pronounced like the *m* in the English word *mother*.

Ng is pronounced like the *ng* in the English word *finger*.

S is pronounced like the *s* in the English word *soup*.

Th is pronounced like the *t* in the English word *tin*.

Tsh is pronounced like the *ch* in the English word *church*.

X is pronounced as a hard, back-of-the-throat *ch*, as in the Scottish word *loch*.

HAUSA

Hausa words are spelled much like your ear hears them and pronunciation of Hausa letters is similar to English pronunciation of the same letters. One major difference is a glottal stop in Hausa, indicated by 'a and 'y. This sound is made deep inside the larynx—almost like a hard *g* sound you make in your throat.

Hausa vowels are pronounced as follows:

a as in *car*

e as in *need*

i as in *eat*

o as in *ocean*

u as in *too*

Hausa consonants are similar to English consonants with these exceptions:

bh as in *barb*

c as in *seat*

dh as in *dark*

f as in *first*

g as in *goat*

h as in *hand*

kh as in car.

A lowercase *r* is pronounced like the *r* in *run*.

A capital *R* is rolled on the tip of the tongue.

S is pronounced as in the word *summer*.

Ts is pronounced as it is in *tsunami*.

Y is pronounced as the *e* in the word *eat*.

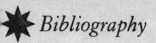

Bibliography

Alexandre, Pierre. *Languages and Language in Black Africa.* Translated by F.A. Leary. Evanston, Illinois: Northwestern University Press, 1972.

Brelin, Christa, ed. *Who's Who Among Black Americans.* Northbrook, IL: Who's Who Among Black Americans, Inc., 1993.

Davidson, Basil. *African Kingdoms.* New York: Time-Life, Inc., 1971.

Dillard, J.L. *Black English.* New York: Random House, 1972.

Doke, Clement Martyn, D. McK. Malcolm, and J.M.A. Sikakana. *English and Zulu Dictionary.* Johannesburg: Witwatersrand University Press, 1958.

Estell, Kenneth, ed. *African America.* Detroit, MI: Visible Ink Press, 1994.

Greenberg, Joseph Harold. *The Languages of Africa.* Bloomington, Indiana: Indiana University Press, 1966.

Guthrie, Malcolm. *The Bantu Languages of Western Equatorial Africa.* London, New York: Published for the International African Institute by Oxford University Press, 1953.

Harrison, Paul Carter. *Black Light, The African American Hero.* New York: Thunder's Mouth Press, 1993.

Inter-territorial Language Committee to the East African Dependencies. *Swahili English Dictionary.* New York: Saphorgraph, 1969.

Lanker, Brian. *I Dream a World.* New York: Stewart, Tabori, and Chang, 1989.

Low, W. Augustus, and Virgil A. Clift, eds. *Encyclopedia of Black America*. New York: Di Capo Press, a subsidiary of Plenum Publishing, 1981.

Mair, Lucy Philip. *African Kingdoms*. Oxford, England: Clarendon Press, 1977.

The New York Times Atlas of the World. New York: Times Books, 1993.

Newman, Roxana Ma. *An English-Hausa Dictionary*. New Haven: Yale University Press, 1990.

Perrott, Daisy Valerie. *Teach Yourself Swahili*. London: English Universities Press, 1957.

Plowden, Martha Ward. *Famous Firsts of Black Women*. Gretna, LA: Pelican Publishing Company, 1993.

Puckett, Newbell Niles. *Black Names in America: Origins and Usage, Collected by Newell Niles Puckett*. Edited by Murray Heller. Boston: G.K. Hall, 1975.

Rechenback, Charles William, assisted by Angelica Wanjinu Gesuga. *Swahili-English Dictionary*. Washington, D.C.: Catholic University of America Press, 1967.

Salley, Columbus. *The Black 100: A Ranking of the Most Influential Americans Past and Present*. New York: Carol Publishing Group, 1993.

Scholefield, Alan. *The Dark Kingdoms: The Impact of White Civilization on Three Great African Monarchies*. New York: William Morrow, 1975.

Shinnie, Margaret. *Ancient African Kingdoms*. New York: New American Library, 1970.

Smith, Jesse Carney. *Black Firsts*. Detroit, MI: Visible Ink Press, 1994.

Smith, Jesse Carney, ed. *Notable Black American Women*. Detroit, MI: Gale Research International Ltd., 1992.

Stevick, Earl W. *Yoruba: A Basic Course*. Washington, D.C.: Department of State, Foreign Service Institute, 1963.

Stevick, Earl W., J.G. Mlela, and F.N. Njenga. *Swahili: A Basic Course*. Washington, D.C.: Department of State, Foreign Service Institute, 1969.

Index

Aabo, 116, 117
Aafin, 115
Aanu, 106, 107, 114
Aaro, 85
Aaron (m), 49
Aasiki, 85
Abafu, 110, 111
Abanidu, 107
Abarba, 145
Abasi, 82
Abayomi, 83
Abdu, 82
Abdullah, 82
Abebi (f), 85
Abejide, 83
Abejunde, 82
Abena (m), 84, 114
Abeokuta, 71
Abethu, 128
Abidjan, 75
Abiola, 83
Abiona, 82
Abo (f), 110
Aboki, 138
Abomey, 71
Abota, 141
Abubakar, 81
Accra, 71, 75

Adaba (f), 109
Adagun, 113
Adalci, 140, 143
Adam (m), 14
Adawole, 104
Ad Dakhla, 77
Addini, 146
Ade, 85
Adeagbo (m), 84
Adebayo (m), 84
Adhana, 93
Adhimu, 96
Adia, 100
Adibu, 103
Adili, 92
Adimika, 101
Adinassi (m), 98
Adio, 83
Adm (m), 2
Aduke, 85
Aduni, 83
Adura, 115
Afeemojumo, 120
Afefe, 105, 106
Afemojumo (f), 108
Afinna, 117
Afiyesi, 119
Afogede, 106

Afojuba, 110
Afomo, 114
Afu, 81
Afya, 81
Agaja (m), 64
Agangan, 117
Agbara, 104, 106, 108,
   113, 115, 119, 121
Agbiro, 118
Agbo, 116
Agbon, 107
Agbonrin, 109
Agidi, 117
Aginju, 121
Agufon, 115
Ahlula, 128, 136
Ahmed, 82
Ahmose-Nefertere (f),
   63
Ahotep (f), 63
Aijebi, 113
Aikata, 89
Aiki, 139
Aisun, 121
Aiye, 109, 120, 122
Aiyetoro, 85
Ajali, 95
Àjamn (m), 84

Names which are not specified as either feminine (f), or masculine (m), can be used for both girls and boys.

Aje, 121
Ajib, 82
Ajodun, 111
Aka, 93
Akeko, 117
Akewi, 115
Akida (m), 93
Akili, 97
Akinlabi (m), 85
Akins (m), 83
Akintunde (m), 83
Akinwunmi, 84
Ako, 83
Akoni, 112
Akowe, 122
Aku, 144
Akuko (m), 117
Ala, 109
Alaabo, 116
Alaafia, 85
Alaanu, 114, 117
Alabapade, 106
Ala (f), 66
Alafia, 112
Alagbara, 104
Alain (m), 31
Alakojo, 111
Alamsiki, 95
Alasaro, 120
Alatu, 143
Albarka, 88
Albert, 73
Alexa (f), 51
Alex (m), 14
Alfahari, 145
Alfajiri (f), 94
Alfarma, 143
Algashi, 145
Alger, 74
Ali, 81
Alice (f), 32, 51, 57
Aliver (m), 5
Aljanna, 144
Alkahura, 147
Almasi (f), 94
Almasihu (m), 144
Almubazzari, 140

Alo, 109
Althea (f), 10, 25
Al'umma, 144
Alusa, 136
Alvin (m), 40
Amachiphiza, 87
Amakha, 125
Amandla, 87, 135
Amani, 99
Amanirenas (f), 62
Ambe, 85
Ameni, 122
Amenirda (f), 63
Amfani, 145
Ami, 107
Amincewa, 148
Aminci, 145
Amini, 104
Aminifu, 101
Amintacce, 148
Amiri (m), 93
Amma (m), 67
Ammu (m), 68
Amotekun, 115, 120
Amsa, 140
Anasa (f), 98
Anchnesmerir (f), 63
Andre (m), 40
Andrew (m), 21
Anelisa, 132
Anfaani, 112, 116
Anga (f), 92, 126
Angaa, 101
Angavu, 93
Angela (f), 29, 43
Angeli (f), 105
Angoi, 71
Angola, 71
Anika, 84
Animashann, 83
Anisi (f), 94
Anita (f), 37, 57
Aniyan, 106, 107
Anjey (f), 1
Annabi, 89
Anna (f), 19
Annashciwa, 144

Ann (f), 48
Annre (f), 3
Ano, 85
Apara, 83
Aparo, 115
Apeje, 120
Apon, 109
Ara, 120
Arabinrin (f), 118
Aradu, 138, 143
Araiye, 114
A Raye, 137
Ardra, 71
Aretha (f), 37
Ariwo, 118
Arohin, 119
Arole, 112
Aroso, 114
Arthur (m), 21, 40, 52, 58
Art (m), 58
Arziki, 146
Arzuta, 88
Asaaju, 114, 115
Asali, 97, 144
Asa (m), 27, 110
Asamale, 119
Asante, 71
Asegun, 108, 121
Asesimba, 85
Aseyori, 119
Ashanti, 69
Ashiki, 98
Asili, 99
Asiri, 146
Askari (m), 103
Askia Muhammad
    Tore (m), 65
Asmara, 75
Aso-Aran, 121
Assalatu (f), 88
Aswan, 75
Atako, 114
Atira (f), 8
Attajiri (m), 137
Atuko (m), 117
Augusta (f), 29, 48

August (m), 34
Aushi, 81
Awada, 111
Awari, 109
Awo, 107
Awodi, 112
Axum, 69
Ayanfe, 110
Aye, 115
Ayinde, 85
Ayize, 87
Ayo, 84
Ayobami, 84
Ayodele, 84
Azali, 95
Azanci, 138
Aziza (f), 81
Azizi, 103
Azurfa, 147

Ba, 137
Baba, 108, 142
Babafemi, 83
Babaza, 122, 130
Babba (m), 137
Babztunde, 83
Baderinwa, 86
Badhirifu, 95
Bado (f), 143, 148
Badru, 80
Baduniye, 149
Bahari, 101
Bahati, 81
Bahatika, 92
Baibia, 92
Ba-Ja, 119
Bakari, 82
Balekela, 135
Bamako, 76
Bambari, 74
Bamvua, 102
Bandele, 82
Bandlulula, 133
Bangui, 74
Bantone (m), 8
Baraka, 92
Baranje, 117

Barazahi, 99
Barbara (f), 19, 25, 48
Barbarasha (f), 3
Barewa, 141
Bariki, 92
Barkwanci, 148
Barone (m), 8
Barubaru, 103
Basira, 88
Bata, 75
Bauna (m), 137
Bavu, 102
Bayana, 103
Bayard (m), 27
Bayo, 85
Bazara, 142
Beah (f), 43
Beauford (m), 49
Behty (f), 1
Beira, 76
Benguela, 70, 71
Benin, 69
Benjamin (m), 14, 27,
    52
Ben (m), 40
Benue, 73
Beresi, 119
Bernard (m), 35
Berry (m), 55
Bertha (f), 25
Bessie (f), 10, 51
Betty (f), 29
Beverly (f), 44
Beyin, 71
Bhacisa, 125
Bheka, 126
Bhekuza (m), 123
Bhelekeqa, 87
Bhensa, 133
Bhodla, 131
Bida, 145
Bi Hakki, 88
Biki, 138, 141
Bilisi, 103
Billie (f), 37
Bill (m), 15, 41, 58
Billy (m), 45

Bil (m), 2
Bilma, 70
Bimkubwa (f), 81
Bingelela, 132
Bissau, 75
Biyayya, 137, 143
Blanche (m), 22
Bobby (m), 27
Bobo-Dioulasso, 74
Boka, 142
Bona, 123
Bonakala, 122
Bonga, 86
Bongoza, 133
Booker (m), 15
Bora, 95
Bori, 115
Bornu, 69
Bosede, 83
Bouake, 75
Boukman (m), 8
Branford (m), 41
Brava, 70
Brazzaville, 74
Breanna (f), 2
Breeze (f), 6
Bryant (m), 35
Bubula, 133
Budurwa (f), 143
Bukun, 105
Bulawayo, 77
Burge, 148
Burtell (m), 4
Busara, 95
Bustani (f), 95
Butha, 123
Butterfly (f), 44
Byron (m), 50

Cabanga, 124
Cacongo, 71
Cairee (f), 1
Cairo, 75
Calvinah (m), 4
Calvin (m), 27
Cameroon, 73
Camille (f), 48, 54

Candace (f), 64
Cannon (m), 6
Cardiss (f), 19
Care, 5
Carl (m), 35
Carmen (f), 37
Carole (f), 33, 44
Carol (f), 19
Carolshay (f), 3
Carolyn (f), 19
Carrie (f), 19
Carter (m), 31
Carversho (m), 4
Casablanca, 76
Cathama, 136
Ceba, 124
Cebedisa (f), 125
Cebengela, 124
Cecil (m), 58
Cediya, 141
Ceto, 139
Chabris (f), 8
Chacha, 102
Chad, 73
Cha (f), 94
Chagina, 93
Chaka, 97
Chamcela, 104
Changamfu, 93
Change, 5
Chansiku, 80
Chante (f), 8
Charaza, 94
Charlayne (f), 33
Charles (m), 15, 22, 35, 41, 50, 58
Charlie (m), 41
Charlotte (f), 29
Charmee (f), 8
Chase (m), 6
Chastity, 5
Cheerful, 5
Cheka, 98
Chigi (f), 102
Chipata, 77
Choice, 6
Chris (m), 45

Chui, 98
Chukwu (m), 68
Chuma (m), 97
Chumu, 96
Cicely (f), 44
Ci-Gaba, 137, 145
Cija, 131
Cimma, 136
Ciyawa, 141
Clairkita (f), 3
Clara (f), 10
Clarence (m), 22, 55
Claude (m), 35
Clementine (f), 48
Cleopatra (f), 64
Cleven (m), 4
Clifford (m), 22
Clifton (m), 31
Clyde (m), 58
Coleman (m), 22
Colin (m), 15
Conakry, 75
Condolence, 6
Condoza, 134
Congo, 71
Constance (f), 10
Constantine, 74
Coretta (f), 25
Cornell (m), 31
Count (m), 41
Courage, 6
Courtesy, 6
Cuango, 73
Cula, 133
Cunene, 73
Curtis (m), 41
Cush, 69
Cyana (f), 8

Dabam, 139
Dabobo, 108, 111
Dada (f), 83, 101
Dafina, 102
Dage, 147
Daidai, 140, 145
Daidaito, 140
Daidaituwa, 88

Daisy (f), 25
Daji, 89
Dakar, 76
Dake, 118
Dalila, 81
Dalji, 103
Da (m), 89
Damina, 145
Damisa, 143
Dan, 118
Daniel (m), 27, 53
Danny (m), 45
Dan'uwa, 137, 139, 143, 147
Danwo, 120
Dara, 109, 111, 112, 119, 121
Daraja, 140, 145, 148, 149
Daraju, 105, 119
Daraya, 114
Dare, 144
Dariji, 111
Darika (m), 137
Dariya, 89
Darleine (f), 1
Daru, 105
Darweshi, 82
Daula, 140
Daurewa, 140
Dave (m), 58
Davera (f), 8
David (m), 22, 53
Davon (m), 8
Dawisu, 144
Dawit (m), 8
Dawwama, 140
Dayomey, 71
Dearness, 6
Debbie (f), 37
Debi (f), 57
Deborah (f), 20
Deedee, 108
De (f), 118
Dejay (m), 3
Delice (m), 8
Demani, 91

Denkyira, 71
Dennis (m), 58
Denzel (m), 46
Dessa (f), 5
Dexter (m), 41
Dhahabu, 96
Dhani, 103
Diahann (f), 11
Diana (f), 37
Didaju, 107
Didakeje, 120
Didara, 112
Dide, 105, 117
Didogba, 110
Didun (f), 108, 119
Dingane, 87
Dini, 101
Dinya, 145
Dionne (f), 37
Djanet, 70
Djenne, 69
Djibouti, 74
Dlala, 129
Dlalisa, 122
Dlamini (m), 65
Dlondlabala, 131
Dlula, 134
Dogara, 139
Dojuko, 107
Donell (m), 4
Dongola, 70
Dongo (m), 67
Don (m), 41
Doris (f), 51
Dorothy (f), 25, 44,
    51
Douala, 74
Douglahs (m), 2
Douglas (m), 22
Dree (m), 8
Dua, 100
Duke (m), 15
Dukiya, 146, 148
Dukushi, 138
Duma, 135
Dun, 115
Duniya, 139, 149

Durojaiye, 85
Dutse (f), 88
Dvonne (f), 5

Earle (m), 46
Earvin (m), 60
Ebo, 117
Ebun, 111
Eda, 108, 110
Eddie (m), 46
Ede (f), 85
Edith (f), 20
Edward (m), 22, 35, 50
Eepo, 118
Efe, 113
Efirin, 114
Efon (m), 106
Efuufu, 121
Egbe, 107, 113
Ehanna, 121
Eiye, 105, 106
Eje, 121
Ekeji, 117
Eko, 109
Ekun, 114
Ekundayo, 85
Eldridge (m), 27
Eleanor (f), 20
Eleda, 108
Elegance, 6
Elegede, 116
Elekeu, 95
Elgon, 73
Elimisha, 102
Elimu, 98
Elizabeth (f), 11, 48,
    49
Ella (f), 25, 37
Ellis (m), 35
Ellison (m), 10
Elmina, 71
Elu, 113
Ema, 96
Embe, 98
Emi, 111, 118
Emi Koussi, 73
Emma (f), 37

Enaba, 131
Enanela, 133
Endesha (f), 26
Enikeji, 107
Enolia (f), 26
Enomwoyi, 85
Enza, 127, 130, 131
Enzakala, 127
Enzi, 100
Eqa, 128
Ere, 117
Erekusu, 113
Erevu, 102
Eric (m), 41
Erin, 114
Ernesta (f), 54
Ernestine (f), 38
Esaba, 87
Eshe, 81
Eshu (m), 67
Eso, 105
Eta-Ina, 118
Ethabisa, 86
Ethemba, 126, 131
Ethembisa, 131
Ethula, 129
Etu, 105
Eua, 100
Eva (f), 26, 38
Ewe, 114
Ewuruku, 107

Faa, 92
Fada, 144
Fadaka, 118
Fadakar, 137
Fada (m), 139
Fadhili, 101
Fafara, 145
Fafaza, 134
Fahali (m), 93
Fahari, 93
Fahimi, 145
Fama, 148
Famora, 113
Fanaka, 100
Fanikiwa, 92

Fannie (f), 26
Fante, 71
Fantsama, 147
Fara'a, 88
Faraja, 80
Faranga (f), 104
Fareti, 144
Farko, 141
Fasaha, 137, 142
Faseha, 100
Fata, 88
Fatiisha, 92
Faye (f), 26
Fayola, 84
Fefe, 100
Femi, 84
Fere, 107
Fifita, 140
Fi-Fun, 120
Fikiri, 100
Finga, 100
Flip (m), 46
Florence (f), 38, 57
Foluke, 84
Forgiveness, 6
Foriti, 115
Franklyn (m), 31
Frank (m), 59
Frederick (m), 15, 31,
    46, 53
Freedom, 6
Freeman (m), 22
Freetown, 76
Fukamela, 124
Fukula, 135
Funa, 132
Fura, 105
Furahi, 92
Fure (f), 137, 141
Futhuzela, 129
Future, 6

Gaba, 129, 130, 141
Gabasi, 109
Gaborone, 74
Gada, 142
Gadina (f), 141

Gagarumi, 141
Gaggafa, 139
Gail (f), 38, 57
Gajimare, 141
Gallane (m), 8
Gambia, 73
Ganiya, 142, 144, 149
Gantalalle, 89
Ganya, 128
Ganye, 143
Gao, 69
Garara, 141
Gardi, 147
Gardner (m), 27
Garka, 144
Garkuwa, 147
Garrett (m), 53
Garydee (m), 4
Gasa, 138
Gashi (f), 88
Gaskiya, 89, 142
Gatanci, 145
Gbadun, 109
Gbadura, 115
Gbekele, 120
Gberaga, 116
Gbile, 111
Gbina, 104
Gbon, 106, 107, 113
Geoffrey (m), 41
George (m), 16, 23, 55,
    59
Georgia (f), 20
Geza, 130
Ghanima, 96
Ghenry (m), 5
Ghiarou, 70
Gida, 142
Giga, 109
Gimbiya (f), 145
Girama, 141
Girba, 146
Girma, 147
Giving, 6
Giwa (m), 140
Gloria (f), 29, 33
Gloriyae (f), 4

Goma, 102
Gondar, 70
Goodness, 6
Gora, 138
Gordon (m), 50
Grace (f), 38
Granville (m), 53
Gregory (m), 41
Guguwa, 148
Gulu, 77
Gumbu, 99
Guy (m), 53
Gwabi, 148
Gwanda, 144
Gwani, 140
Gwaninta, 140
Gwara (f), 147
Gwarzo (m), 89
Gwendolyn (f), 11, 33
Gxila, 134
Gyara, 142

Haba, 94
Hada, 142
Hadari, 147
Hadhi, 101
Hadiya, 81
Haeroeld (m), 2
Haiba (f), 92
Haihuwa, 137
Hakika, 146
Hakikance, 88
Hakunci, 143
Halala, 122
Hali, 138
Halitta, 139
Halle (f), 44
Hallie (f), 30
Hamba, 127, 135
Hamdu, 100
Hami, 100
Hamidi, 80
Hammer (m), 6
Hamu, 92
Hankali, 138, 143, 145,
    146
Hank (m), 16

Hapu, 112
Harare, 77
Hargeisa, 76
Harold (m), 23
Harriet (f), 11
Harry (m), 42
Hasani (m), 81
Hashaza, 132
Hasina, 81
Haska, 147
Haskaka, 142
Haske, 143
Hathor (f), 67
Hatsabibi, 89
Hatshepsut (f), 64
Hattie (f), 44
Hawula, 135
Hayiya, 86
Hazaka, 137
Hazbiya, 148
Hazel (f), 20
Hazo, 89
Hekima, 104
Helene (f), 51
Heluma (m), 142
Henry (m), 31
Herschel (m), 59
Hibibu, 92
Hihan, 119
Hikaya, 140
Hikima, 89
Himma, 139
Hisani, 98
Hlakanipha, 125
Hlangabeza, 87
Hlantula, 132
Hlonipha, 126
Hlubuka, 131
Hodari, 100
Homer (m), 16
Honor, 6
Houis (m), 5
Houston (m), 31
Hua, 104
Hukunci, 139
Hulaza, 131
Huluki, 94

Hunturu, 138
Huwa, 105

Ibadan, 71, 76
Ibasepo, 108
Ibeji, 120
Ibere, 111
Ibheji, 124
Ibi, 105
Ibowo, 117
Ibrahim (m), 89
Ibukun, 105
Ibura, 98
Ice (m), 6
Ida (f), 11
Idajo, 113
Idakekeje, 120
Idake-Roro, 117
Idan, 114
Idapo, 110
Idawoduro, 111
Idi, 109, 111, 116
Idiji, 107
Idite, 113
Ife, 84
Ifetayo, 84
Ifihan, 116
Ifiyesi, 116
Ifonahan, 112
Iforiti, 115, 119
Igba, 117
Igbadun, 114
Igbagbo, 110
Igbala, 108, 117
Igberaga, 115
Igbeyawo, 121
Igbo, 71
Igboiya, 106, 111, 116
Ihlakahiphile, 86
Ijade-Lo, 110
Ijaro, 114, 117
Iji, 119, 120
Ijo, 108
Ikede, 116
Ikekuru, 109
Ikera, 120
Iko, 138

Ikuphakama, 124
Ikuukuu, 107
Ileri, 116
Ilhami, 142
Ilibhabha (m), 133
Ilibheleba (m), 134
Ilibhilikosa, 122
Iliconsi, 124
Ilidlingozi, 128
Ilifa, 126
Ilifefe, 123
Ilifuba, 129
Iligama, 133
Iligeza (m), 125
Iligubhela, 129
Iligugu, 126, 135
Iligwinci, 136
Ilihalandanda, 130
Ilihlathi, 87
Ilihlosi, 128
Ilihobhe (f), 135
Ilijele, 126
Ilikhaneli, 123
Ilikhasi, 126
Ilikhaya, 126
Ilikhwalithi, 131
Iliklume, 136
Ilikomkhulu, 132
Ililala, 128
Ililanga, 134
Ililungelo, 130
Ilimi, 143
Ilinqomfi, 126
Ilioki, 127
Iliphalasi, 128
Ilipharadisi, 128
Iliphathi, 128
Iliphera, 129
Ilipigogo, 129
Ilipulamu, 129
Iliqholosha, 134
Iliqiniso, 135
Iliroza (f), 132
Ilisasa, 127
Ilishinga, 131
Ilistelingi, 134
Ilithanga, 130

Ilithayiga, 135
Ilithemba, 124
Ilithendele, 128
Ilithuba, 128
Ilitilosi (m), 132
Ilizi, 93
Ilizibu (f), 136
Ilizulu, 133
Ilorin, 71
Imamu (m), 35
Imani, 88
Imara, 102
Imbali (f), 123
Imbudle, 125
Imelika, 135
Imfanelo, 124, 130
Imfezi, 123
Imhotep (m), 65
Imo, 110, 113, 120
Imole, 114
Imotele, 111
Imototo, 107
Impekumpeku, 135
Impophoma, 136
Imuse, 111
Imvula, 131
Ina, 107, 111
Inakuna, 110
Incembe (f), 135
Incwelana, 129
Indle, 136
Indlela, 134
Indluzula, 125
Indodakazi (f), 124
Indodana (m), 133
Induduzo, 124
Induna (m), 127
Ingane, 123
Ingarma (m), 147
Ingclungulu, 135
Ingewepheshi, 123
Ingijimi, 135
Inglebo, 131
Ingoibi (m), 87
Ingonyama, 126
Ingqondo, 126, 131
Ingwejeje, 134

Inhianhla, 127
Inhlanhlana, 134
Inhliziyo, 130, 136
Inhlonipho, 131
Injabulo, 86
Injaka, 124
Injitimane (m), 125
Inkabi, 128
Inkangakusa, 87
Inkani, 132
Inkazimulo, 125
Inkondlo, 129
Inkosikazi (m), 126
Inkosi, 87
Inkungu, 127
Inkuthalo, 136
Inkwindi, 87
Innocence, 6
Inqaba, 129
Inqama, 131
Insindiso, 131
Insini, 87
Intambiso, 129
Intobeko, 126
Intwasahlobo, 134
Inuwa, 146
Inyamazane, 122
Inyanga, 127
Inyoni, 123
Inyosi, 86
Inzalamizi (m), 129
Iparada, 106
Ipasan, 115
Ira (m), 42
Iran, 121
Irapada, 116
Irawo, 119
Irele, 113
Irepo, 112
Ireti, 113
Iridi, 108
Irili, 146
Iro, 110, 113
Iroju, 109
Irole, 110
Irora, 118
Isami, 105

Isandla, 123
Isanzwili, 127
Ise, 104
Isele, 109
Ishmael (m), 35
Isibindi, 124, 130, 134
Isibusiso, 86
Isichibi, 130
Isifiki, 127
Isigijimi, 122, 132
Isihlanhlathi, 86
Isihlanjana, 87
Isihluphe (f), 86
Isijabuli, 134
Isijibo, 109
Isikhotha, 135
Isikhova, 128
Isikhulu, 86
Isikhulukazi (f), 87
Isiko, 121
Isilisa (m), 127
Isiluba, 125
Isilwi, 86
Isimangaliso, 124, 127
Isimo, 123
Isin, 106, 116
Isingane (f), 135
Isinqumelo, 124
Isinyelela, 134
Isiphepho, 124, 136
Isiphiwo, 135
Isipho, 87
Isiqholiso, 126
Isiqhwaga (m), 134
Isiqondo, 131
Isiqu, 131
Isisa, 125
Isis (f), 66
Isithunzi, 129
Isivamelo, 130
Isivunguzane, 132
Isizotha, 129
Isizwe, 127
Iska, 137, 148
Ismenie (f), 63
Isoji, 117
Isoka, 122

Isokan, 107
Issa, 81
Isun, 111
Isura, 120
Itakun, 113
Itan, 110, 112
Itansan, 112
Itara, 122
Itifaki, 96
Itiju, 105
Itunu, 107, 108
Ituri (f), 96
Iva (f), 4
Iwa, 106, 116, 146
Iwaasu, 117
Iwin, 109, 110, 115
Iya, 138
Iyalenu, 105
Iyanju, 109
Iyanu, 114, 119, 122
Iyara, 110, 118
Iyato, 109
Iyawa, 136, 147
Iyaye, 140
Iye, 110, 113, 121
Iyebiye, 115
Iyigugu (f), 125
Iyin, 105, 107, 115
Iyonu, 122
Iyun, 108
Izibuko, 131
Izigalo, 123
Izinhloni, 127

Ja, 146
Jaali, 92
Jabari, 81
Jabulela, 124
Jabulisa, 86
Jackie (f), 57
Jackie (m), 16, 45, 59
Jack (m), 59
Jadean (m), 3
Jaha, 81
Jahi, 81
Jahina, 93
Jaims (m), 2

Jajaime (m), 3
Jaju (m), 7
Jamaaldeen (m), 4
Jamala, 100
Jamal (m), 7
James (m), 16, 28, 35,
    46, 50, 59, 60
Jamesone (m), 4
Jamila (f), 80
Jamin (m), 7
Jamon (m), 7
Janal (m), 7
Janeel (m), 7
Jane (f), 20, 51
Janet (f), 38
Janie (f), 30
Jantu (m), 7
Jaquin, 71
Jarain (m), 7
Jareem (m), 7
Jarumi, 88
Jaruntaka, 137, 139,
    148
Jasmine (f), 44
Jatherine (f), 4
Javin (m), 7
Javo (m), 7
Jawa, 146
Jaye (m), 46
Jean (m), 17
Jeejee (f), 118
Jelani, 81
Jenne, 70
Jesey (m), 2
Jesse (m), 17, 31, 59
Jessye (f), 38
Jewel (f), 6
Jewell (f), 20, 30
Ji, 144
Jihadi, 139
Jijadu, 107
Jima, 75
Jimi (m), 42
Jinaki, 103
Jini, 137
Jinjina, 138, 146
Jinle, 116

Jioni, 97
Jito, 101
Joan (f), 54
Joba, 116
Joe (m), 32, 59
Joezer (m), 8
Jogun, 113
Johari (f), 98
John (m), 23, 28, 36,
    42, 46, 50, 55
Johnnetta (f), 30
Joie (f), 44
Jokha, 82
Jonathan (m), 55
Josephine (f), 11
Joseph (m), 23, 28
Joshi, 101
Josoya (f), 8
Jua, 102
Juanita (f), 38
Juba, 73, 77
Jubalala, 134
Judgment, 6
Judith (f), 38
Julie (f), 45
Julius (m), 59
Jumoke, 84
Jumu, 98
Justina (f), 52
Juya, 147

Kaa, 91
Kaabo, 121
Kabaila, 100
Kabewa, 145
Kabwe, 77
Kada, 137, 139
Kadai, 137
Kaddara, 139, 140
Kaharabu, 91
Kahina (f), 64
Kai, 137
Kaifi, 147
Kailula, 147
Kaka, 141
Kakamia, 104
Kakhulu, 128

Kalala, 97
Kalamka, 92
Kalo (f), 143
Kalubalanta, 139
Kamaria, 81
Kambi, 139
Kammala, 148
Kamnandi, 129
Kampala, 77
Kancane, 133
Kangara, 139
Kani, 95
Kankan, 75
Kankara, 147
Kano, 71, 76
Kanshi (f), 141
Kanu, 104
Kanya, 140
Kanzi, 97
Kapaza, 127
Kara, 88
Karama, 95
Karammiski, 148
Karamu, 95
Kararrawa, 137
Kareem (m), 59
Karfi, 89
Kari, 146
Kariba, 73, 77
Karibisho, 103
Karimci, 88
Karimi, 138
Karisimbi, 73
Karkara, 138
Karole (f), 1
Karu, 143
Karuwa, 88
Kasa, 138, 142
Kasabu, 93
Kasai, 73
Kasaita, 89
Kasashen, 142
Kaskazi, 99
Kassala, 77
Katherine (f), 39
Kathleen (f), 39
Katiti (f), 103

Katunga, 69
Kauci, 144
Kaunata, 143
Kawance, 138
Kayatar, 88
Ke, 117
Keely (m), 8
Kehinde, 85
Kenneth (m), 56
Kenshay (m), 4
Kere, 120
Kereng'ende, 94
Keresimesi, 107
Keta, 71
Ketare, 139
Keya (m), 8
Khala, 133
Khalfani, 81
Khanya, 133
Khartoum, 77
Khifiza, 134
Khonsa, 130
Khula, 135
Khulula, 132
Khuluma, 133
Khunsela, 134
Khuthazela, 129
Kiafrika, 91
Kiana (f), 4
Kibibi (f), 82
Kibuku (m), 67
Kiburi, 91
Kibwana (m), 95
Kichea, 93
Kida, 144
Kidaka, 93
Kidani (f), 99
Kidimu, 104
Kidomo (f), 94
Kigogo, 102
Kike (f), 95
Kiki, 112
Kikora, 101
Kikuti, 99
Kilimanjaro, 73
Kilwa, 69
Kimalidadi, 95

Kimera (m), 65
Kimeta, 100
Kimya, 93
Kina, 96
Kinaya, 101
King (m), 6
Kiniun, 114
Kinokero, 96
Kinshasa, 77
Kintu (m), 65
Kinyamkela, 104
Kinyemi, 102
Kipenzi, 95
Kipepo (f), 96
Kipupwe, 94
Kipure (f), 94
Kirby (m), 60
Kirfa, 138
Kirimu, 92
Kirinyaga, 73
Kirki, 89
Kiroho, 102
Kirumbizi, 96
Kisikusiku, 103
Kisiri, 101
Kisumu, 75
Kisura (f), 100
Kita, 92
Kititi, 94
Kito (f), 100
Kitoma, 102
Kitukuu, 96
Kitwana, 82
Kiumbo, 93
Kiva, 103
Kivuno, 97
Kiwimbi, 101
Kizingo, 101
Kizushi, 97
Klomela, 87
Ko-Eko, 114
Kogi, 146
Kokoro, 106
Kokumuo, 85
Kolokolo, 111
Komanya, 98
Korama, 89

Kore, 116
Korin, 106, 118
Koya, 148
Kucha, 94
Kudura, 98
Kufula, 141
Kukula, 95
Kullum, 138
Kumasi, 70, 71, 75
Kumbi-Saleh, 70
Kumekuchwa, 102
Kuna, 142
Kunge, 98
Kunle, 84
Kunna, 143
Kunya, 144
Kupanda, 100
Kurmi, 148
Kuro (m), 103
Kurt (m), 23
Kurwa, 147
Kusuru, 103
Kuti, 98
Kuu, 94
Kuzari, 136, 140, 147, 148
Kwalwa, 147
Kwamanda (m), 138
Kwanya, 137
Kwarjini, 141, 145
Kwasakwasa, 144
Kwasi, 92
Kwazo, 149
Kweli, 103
Kwenzi (f), 102
Kweupe, 93
Kwini (f), 100
Kyakkyawa, 88
Kyanwa, 138
Kyau, 88
Kyauta, 88

Laabu, 91
La'andra (f), 7
Laayoune, 77
Labalaba, 106
Lada, 146

Ladabi, 139, 144, 145, 148
Ladawn (f), 2
Ladi, 118
Ladonna (f), 2, 7
Lafiya, 88
Lafua, 92
Lagbara, 114, 115, 121
Laghouat, 74
Lagos, 71, 76
Laiberu, 121
Laidojuko, 120
Laifoiya, 110
Laigbonran, 112
Lailai, 110
Lailese, 118
Lailewu, 117
Laini (f), 94
Lainiwon, 120
Laisabawon, 121
Laiteju, 117
Laiya, 105, 106, 108, 119
Lake (m), 6
Lalela, 87
Lambarene, 75
Lamontel (m), 4
Lamula, 127
Langston (m), 36
Laniva (f), 7
Laniyan, 120
Larenz (m), 8
Larita (f), 7
Lashaina (f), 7
Lashandra (f), 7
Lashanta (f), 7
Lasue (f), 3
Latanda (f), 7
Latasha (f), 7
Latifah (f), 7, 12
Latifu, 96
Latina (f), 7
Latoya (f), 7
Laurence (m), 46
La Var (m), 46
Laveena (f), 7
Lawanda (f), 7

Layo, 113
Layvonne (f), 7
Leandrea (f), 2
Lee (m), 60
Leke, 120
Leleejah (f), 8
Lena (f), 39
Lenu, 106
Leon (m), 32
Leontyne (f), 39
Lepa, 116
LeRoi (m), 35
Lerose (f), 3
Leroy (m), 61
Leshi, 143
Leslie (f), 39
Lewa, 105, 110, 115
Lewis (m), 53
Leza (m), 67
Lichinga, 76
Likita, 139, 145
Likizo, 97
Lillian (f), 39
Limpopo, 73
Linjila, 137
Lisata (f), 4
Liwaza, 93
Lixubungu, 126
Loango, 71
Lobito, 74
Logbon, 118
Lokanjuwa, 105
Lokiki, 115
Lola, 111, 112
Lome, 77
Londa, 130
Londoloza, 130
Lonii, 120
Lorene (f), 33
Lorraine (f), 12
Louis (m), 23, 42, 47
Loye, 117
Lualaba, 73
Luanda, 71, 74
Lubumbashi, 77
Lucy (f), 30, 33
Lulu (f), 82

Lumana, 89
Lunga, 86
Lungisa, 132
Lusaka, 77
Lu'ulu'u (f), 139

Maabudu, 101
Maadhimisho, 93
Maceci, 146
Mace (f), 89
Macheo, 102
Machwa, 102
Madahiro, 96
Madhubuti, 97
Mae (f), 12
Mafaka, 147
Mafanikio, 102
Mafarki, 139
Mafifici, 148
Magaji, 142
Magani, 146
Magariba, 148
Maggie (f), 12
Magglean (f), 4
Magic (m), 60
Mahaba, 91
Mahalia (f), 12
Mahiri, 101
Maisha, 98
Majaliwa, 98
Makao, 97
Makasudi, 144
Makeda (f), 63
Makini, 102
Mala'ika (f), 137
Malaika (f), 91
Malanje, 74
Malcolm (m), 17
Mali, 70
Malindi, 70, 71
Manan, 71
Mangalisa, 123
Manyonyota, 95
Manzili, 102
Mapendezi, 96
Maputo, 76
Maraice, 140

Mararki, 139
Marcus (m), 17
Margaret (f), 33, 49
Marguerite (f), 30
Marian (f), 12, 26
Maridhia, 93
Mario (m), 47
Mariwo, 111
Marjani, 80
Marmari, 88
Marrakech, 76
Marsha (f), 45
Marshall (m), 60
Martin (m), 17
Marubuci, 149
Marva (f), 30
Marvin (m), 42
Mary (f), 13, 20, 21,
  48, 52
Masahaba (m), 94
Masallata, 138
Maseru, 75
Mashahuri, 140
Mashi, 89
Masud, 81
Matabbaci, 89
Matafiyi, 148
Matamalaki, 101
Matarajio, 97
Matsa, 147
Matthew (m), 18
Matuko, 93
Mauguzi, 93
Maume (m), 98
Maundifu, 103
Mavunde, 99
Mawaki, 145, 147
Mawimbi, 102
Mawu (m), 67, 68
Maxine (f), 13
Max (m), 36
Maya (f), 33
May (f), 52
Maynard (m), 23
Mayungiyungi (f), 103
Mazakuta (m), 89
Mazo, 137

Mbabane, 77
Mbalamwezi, 99
Mbari, 95
Mbingu, 102
Mbita, 80
Mbobo, 91
Mbwana (m), 81
Mchekeshi, 98
Mdalasini, 93
Mdambi, 96
Mdarabi, 101
Mdirifu, 103
Medgar (m), 28
Meka, 95
Melissah (f), 2
Memetuko (f), 101
Mer-Neith (f), 63
Meroe, 70
Meru, 73
Meshach (m), 47
Meta, 94
Metalokan, 120
Mfalme (m), 101
Mfariji, 94
Mfasa, 96
Mfululizo, 101
Mfurahivu, 96
Mhenga, 99
Mhina (f), 81
Michael (m), 23, 60
Mike (m), 60
Mikul (m), 2
Milas (m), 5
Miles (m), 42
Mimo, 112, 117
Mimora, 110
Mjenzi (m), 93
Mjibu, 100
Mkalimu, 103
Mkwao, 95
Mlimwengu, 97
Mnyofu, 97
Mo, 109, 119
Modupe, 84
Mogrant (m), 3
Molefi (m), 32
Molemole, 106

Moms (f), 45
Monamona, 114
Monrovia, 75
Montague (m), 53
Montel (m), 47
Mordecai (m), 32
Morgan (m), 47
Mosi, 81
Moto, 95
Moundou, 74
Moyo, 97
Mpaji, 96
Mpasi, 96
Mpekuzi, 97
Mpendwa, 104
Mpoa, 94
Mpumelele, 87
Mpwa, 99
Mrashi (f), 99
Mratabu, 100
Msadikifu, 103
Msalihina, 97
Msambale (f), 95
Msamehaji, 96
Mtendaji, 95
Mtini, 95
Mtukufu, 101
Mtukutu, 98
Mtumbuizi, 99
Mtutumo, 102
Muawana, 97
Muhammad (m), 60
Muhimmi, 88
Mulukiya, 144
Mulungu (m), 67
Murdede (m), 144
Murfu, 142
Murjani, 138
Murna, 138, 139, 143
Murua, 96
Musafaha, 141
Musa (m), 68
Mutemwia (f), 63
Mutesa (m), 65
Mutum (m), 144
Mutunci, 88, 142
Muumba, 99

Muzakkari, 140
Muziki, 99
Mvuvi (m), 95
Mwabudu, 104
Mwaguzi, 102
Mwali, 99
Mwalimu, 101
Mwamana, 99
Mwamini, 82
Mwamua, 99
Mwanachewa, 91
Mwanachuo, 99
Mwanamaji (m), 101
Mwanasesere (f), 94
Mwanathaura, 101
Mwandani, 93
Mwandishi, 104
Mwangwi, 95
Mwanza, 77
Mwanzilishi, 100
Mwaridi (f), 101
Mwazaji, 97
Mwelewa, 100
Mwendelezi, 99
Mwenzi, 96
Mweru, 73
Mweza, 99
Mwezi, 98
Mwindaji (m), 97
Mwinyi (m), 81
Mwongezi, 95
Mwujiza, 102
Mwungwana, 96
Mzeituni, 99
Mzuzi, 97

Nace, 89
Naci, 142
Nadan (m), 3
Nadiri, 145
Nafsi, 93
Nagari, 148
Nagarta, 139, 141
Nairobi, 75
Naka, 135
Nambawani, 103
Namiji (m), 144

Nanaa, 98
Nannga, 91
Naomi (f), 55
Nasara, 148
Nashia, 101
Nassor, 82
Natalie (f), 39
Naula (f), 5
Nawiri, 96
Nayo, 86
Ndonda (f), 130
Neema, 80
Neemevu, 100
Nefertiti (f), 63
Neith (f), 67
Neith-Hotep (f), 63
Nell (f), 57
Nema, 146
Nemsi, 97
Neqiniso (m), 124
Ngaphandle, 126
Ngempela, 130
Ngesibindi, 123
Ngewo (m), 68
Nginamandla, 86
Ngiyindoda (m), 86
Ngothando, 126
Nguru, 76
Nguu, 99
Ngwane (m), 65
Ngwena, 94
Nia, 5, 96
Niamey, 76
Niani, 71
Niara (f), 30
Ni-Didaraya, 119
Nifaiya, 121
Nife, 108
Niger, 73
Ni-Iwa, 111
Nika, 110, 130
Nikoko, 117
Nile, 73
Nina (f), 39
Nipinnu, 108
Nirokuro, 110
Nironu, 118

Nisegun, 121
Nishadi, 141
Nishell (f), 3
Nitara, 109
Nitiju, 105
Nitocris (f), 63
Nitooto, 120
Nitsuwa, 138
Niwa (m), 119
Niyanu, 119
Niyelori, 122
Niye-Meji, 117
Niyin, 104
Nla, 105
Nomalanga, 87
Nong'ona, 104
Norma (f), 49
Nouakchott, 76
Nowina, 87
Nqokuthula, 126
Ntozake (f), 33
Ntwela (f), 86
Numfashi, 137
Nuru, 80
Nyambe (m), 68
Nyasa, 73
Nyati, 93
Nyeta, 92
Nyoka, 92
Nzigunzigu (f), 93
Nzinga A Knuwu (m),
     65
Nzingha (f), 64

Oba (m), 65, 84
Obataiye (m), 84
Obinrin (f), 121
Obuko (m), 106
Octavia (f), 33
Odam (m), 5
Ode, 85
Odetta (f), 39
Odo, 117
Ododo (f), 111
Oduduwa (m), 65
Ofundayo, 131
Ogagun, 106

Ogba, 111
Ogbeni (m), 118
Ogbon, 105, 109, 116,
     119, 121
Ogo, 112
Ogun (m), 68, 112, 114
Ohlambayo, 135
Oidah, 71
Ojeun, 121
Ojiji, 118
Ojo, 116
Okan, 112
Okavango, 73
Okera, 84
Okholwayo, 86
Okiki, 110, 116
Okubikwe, 130
Okujabulisayo, 87
Okun, 115, 117
Okunakisayo, 126
Okuningi, 129
Okunrin (m), 114
Okuta-Iyebiye (f), 113
Ola, 108, 113
Olabishi, 84
Olafemi, 84
Olaju, 107
Olaniyan, 84
Olaniyi, 85
Olatunde, 84
Olivia (f), 30
Olododo, 85
Olofin, 114
Ologbo, 106
Ologbon, 115, 117
Ologose, 118
Ologun (m), 121
Olokubonga, 135
Olola, 108
Oloore-Ofe, 112
Olooto, 110
Olorun (m), 68, 108
Olote, 116
Olotito, 120, 121
Olotunde, 83
Oloye, 106, 111
Olubayo, 84

Olufe, 105, 108, 111
Olufemi, 83
Olufunke, 83
Olufunmilayo, 83
Olufunni, 111
Olugbala, 85
Oluko, 120
Olukun (m), 68
Oluranlowo, 112
Oluse, 109
Olushegun, 84
Olushola, 83
Olusin, 122
Olusora, 121
Olutoju, 112
Olutosin, 83
Oluyemi, 83
Omiran, 111
Omnira, 114
Omoge (f), 113
Omokunrin (m), 118
Omolangi (f), 109
Omolara, 83
Omo-Ologbo (f), 113
Omo-Omo, 112
Onde, 106
Onigbagbo, 105, 107
Onigbe, 121
Onigoolu, 112
Oninure, 106
Onitiju (f), 108
Onitsha, 76
Oniyelori, 121
Oogun, 111
Oorun, 119
Ope, 112
Opin, 112
Opo, 104, 105
Opobo, 71
Opolopo, 115
Oprah (f), 13
Orange, 73
Oranyan (m), 65
Ore, 107, 111
Orenthal (m), 60
Orin, 118
Oro, 86

Ororo (f), 103
Oru, 115
Orun, 118
Osahar, 83
Osai Tutu (m), 66
Osan, 108
Osanyin (m), 68
Osayaba, 83
Oscar (m), 23
Oseye, 84
Oso, 104, 109
Osooro, 106
Osoro, 119
Osumare, 116
Osupa, 114
Ota, 94
Ote, 122
Oteo, 97
Othwebulayo, 86
Otis (m), 42
Otito, 112, 113, 120
Otutu, 107, 111
Ougadougou, 74
Owasindayo, 134
Owenzayo, 129
Owo, 116
Owuro, 119
Oye, 113
Oyin, 113
Oyo, 71
Ozifunelayo, 132

Pacha, 99
Pagao, 91
Pamia (f), 4
Papa, 114
Papio, 97
Parakou, 74
Pase, 120
Pataki, 113
Patience, 6
Patricia (f), 21
Patrick (m), 60
Paule (f), 34
Pauli (f), 26
Paul (m), 36, 47, 50, 56
Pe, 119

Pearl (f), 40
Pembea, 102
Pendekezo, 104
Pendeleo, 96
Penyenye, 101
Pepo, 102
Percy (m), 54, 56
Peremende, 99
Pese, 116
Phandla, 123, 124
Phanquza, 122
Phaphalaza, 134
Phatha, 125
Phila Kahle, 126
Phoebe (f), 49
Phonsa, 133
Phran (f), 1
Phukuthisa, 133
Phuma, 131
Phumelela, 134
Phumsesela, 133
Phylicia (f), 45
Piety, 6
Pili, 82
Pinnu, 116
Pipalo, 114
Pipe, 115
Pipon, 114
Pirikana (m), 99
Pon, 118
Pongezi, 94
Pooyi, 121
Pora (m), 104
Pori, 104
Pretoria, 77
Pride, 6
Prince (m), 6
Probity, 6
Puma, 92
Pupa, 116
Pupo, 115
Purupuru, 100

Qananaza, 132
Qaphaza, 129
Qaphela, 135
Qaza, 132

Qhakaza (f), 125
Qhama, 134
Qhuba, 124
Qoqana, 124
Queen (f), 6
Quincy (m), 42
Quinisa, 134

Raba, 146
Rabat, 76
Radhi, 96
Radhiya, 80
Rafiki (m), 94
Rago, 145
Raha, 100
Rahimu, 98
Rai, 97, 143, 148
Rakel (f), 2
Ralph (m), 18, 28, 36
Ramisi, 95
Ramla, 82
Ramona (f), 26
Rana, 148
Randall (m), 28
Rangi, 93
Rani, 139
Ranlowo, 108
Rashida, 82
Rasuli, 100
Ravon (m), 4
Rawa, 139
Rayu, 148
Rayuwa, 140
Rebecca (f), 52
Redd (m), 47
Reggie (m), 60
Reginald (m), 56, 60
Rehema, 81
Rekoja, 110, 119
Rele, 106
Rere, 105
Reriin, 113, 118
Resolution, 6
Respect, 6
Riba, 141
Richard (m), 36,
    47

Riddick (m), 8
Rin, 121
Rina, 142
Rindima, 101
Rine, 139
Riro, 119
Rita (f), 34
Ro, 113
Robert (m), 18, 24, 27, 56, 61
Roburt (m), 2
Rock (m), 6
Rogbodiyan, 110
Roho, 102
Roku, 94
Roland (m), 54
Romare (m), 50
Ronald (m), 24, 54
Ronnelly (m), 5
Ronu, 108
Ronupiwada, 116
Ropo, 119
Roro, 111
Rosa (f), 13
Roy (m), 28, 42
Ruby (f), 45
Rufano, 81
Rufisque, 71
Rukiya (f), 82
Rukwa, 73
Runguma, 140, 142
Runhu, 138
Rura, 146
Ruwa, 145
Ruwe, 105

Sa'a, 143
Sabha, 75
Sabo, 141, 144
Sabunta, 146
Sadaka, 138
Sadifu, 92
Sadiki, 81
Safi, 80
Safiya, 144
Sage, 6
Sahra (f), 81

Saka, 93, 106
Saki, 89
Sakitu, 104
Salama, 103
Salee (f), 2
Salihi, 99
Saliim, 82
Salla, 145
Salma, 82
Saludae (f), 8
Sama, 142, 147
Sambamba, 101
Samellaa (f), 8
Sammy (m), 43
Samori Ibu Lafiya (m), 66
Samu, 136, 148
Samuel (m), 54
Sanaga, 73
Sani, 143
Sansani, 138
Santiea (f), 8
Sarabi, 98
Sarah (f), 40, 55
Sarakai, 144
Sarauniya (f), 145
Sarauta, 146
Sare (m), 97
Satchel (m), 61
Savita (f), 8
Scott (m), 43
Segun, 107, 121
Sekou Tore (m), 66
Selege, 108
Selma (f), 49
Senegal, 73
Septima (f), 26
Serowe, 74
Seyyedia, 98
Sha'awa, 136, 140
Shababu, 102
Shabeelle, 73
Shabill (m), 3
Shagilia, 103
Shahara, 146
Shaho, 141
Shaka (m), 66

Shamba (m), 66
Shamla (f), 8
Shandy (f), 8
Shango (m), 68
Shapat (m), 3
Shaquille (m), 61
Shari'a, 143
Sharmba (m), 8
Sharon (f), 14
Sharufa, 81
Shashawna (f), 3
Shatom (m), 3
Shauki, 140
Shawara, 137
Shela, 128
Shenakdakhete (f), 63
Shepenepout (f), 63
Shepenoupet (f), 63
Sherian (f), 21
Sherlon (m), 8
Shikashikeka, 136
Shiri, 142
Shirley (f), 14, 52
Shiru, 145, 147
Shirya, 137
Shisa, 133
Shomari, 81
Shugaba, 89
Shugabanta, 143
Shujaa (m), 97
Shukuma, 80
Shukuza, 134
Shupavu, 103
Sibu, 95
Sidney (m), 24, 47
Sifuri, 94
Sihiri, 95
Sijilmasa, 71
Sika, 123
Sike, 106
Sikio, 98
Simba, 81
Singatha, 125
Sinzia, 94
Sippie (f), 40
Sismanga, 103
Siso, 108

Sisokunkun, 109
Sitawi, 98
Sithibeza, 127
Siti (f), 81
Siza, 123
Smokey (m), 43
Sobeknofru (f), 63
Sobriety, 6
Sofala, 71
Sofofo, 121
Soga (m), 92
Soja, 118, 147
Sojourner (f), 14
Somode, 122
Songhai, 70
Sonia (f), 34
Soosi, 107, 119
Sooto, 114, 118
Sopo, 120
Sora, 106
Soro, 107
Soza, 91
Spike (m), 6, 47
Stahika, 92
Stahimilivu, 100
Stakimu, 103
Star (f), 6
Steev (m), 2
Stephen (m), 28,
  50
Stevie (m), 43
Stokely (m), 28
Storm (m), 6
Subira, 82
Suga, 119
Sukari, 102, 148
Sumbata, 143
Sumul, 147
Suna, 140, 141
Sundjata (m), 66
Sunshine (f), 6
Susan (f), 34
Suuru, 115
Suzun (f), 2
Swabuluka, 87

Taadhima, 96

Taadhimika, 92
Taanasa, 98
Taara, 109
Taba, 140
Tabahani, 92
Tabaruki, 96
Tabiri, 103
Tabora, 77
Tafiya, 89
Taghaza, 71
Tagulla, 138
Tahyati, 97
Taibu, 92
Taiwo, 85
Takedda, 71
Takoradi, 75
Taliki, 140
Tamata (f), 140
Tamba, 94
Tambo, 103
Tambuzi, 97
Tan, 109, 116, 120
Tana, 73
Tanadhari, 92
Tanda (f), 148
Tandawaa, 92
Tanga, 77
Tangambili, 100
Tanganyika, 73
Tanna, 105
Tano (m), 68
Tasawari, 93
Tashi, 88
Tashibi, 100
Tatsuniya, 140, 141
Tatu, 82
Taura (f), 5
Tauraruwa, 147
Tausayi, 89
Taushi, 147
Tawasufi, 100
Ta-Wsret (f), 63
Tayarisha, 98
Tayo, 110
Teere, 118
Tego, 98
Teku, 144, 146

Telorun, 112
Tembo (m), 95
Temitope, 85
Tenacity, 6
Tenee (f), 8
Tengamaji, 103
Terry (f), 34
Tesuba, 117
Tete, 71, 109
Tevin (m), 5
Thabana-Ntlenyana,
  73
Thanda, 87
Thandaza, 132
Thandisisa, 122
Thelonious (m), 43
Themba, 87
Thembisa, 125
Thomas (m), 24, 36, 56
Thulisa, 128
Thurgood (m), 18
Thyrann (f), 8
Timbuktu, 70
Tinubu (f), 64
Tisa, 119
Titakiti, 118
Titilayo, 84
Tito, 108
Tiye (f), 63
Tobi, 107, 112, 114
Tobisa, 133
Toeney (m), 2
Tolani (f), 8
Tombouctou, 76
Tonald (m), 5
Toni (f), 34
Tony (m), 36
Toogbe, 109, 118
Torkwase (f), 85
Torr (m), 8
Toubakal, 73
Tracarl (m), 3
Traney (m), 8
Trebecca (f), 5
Trevlin (m), 8
Triallen (m), 3
Triellen (f), 3

Tripoli, 75
Trudo Audati (m), 66
Tsanani, 146
Tsare, 139
Tsarki, 142, 145, 146
Tsawa, 148
Tsayayye, 89
Tshekula, 125
Tsibiri, 142
Tsigi, 143
Tsinkaya, 141
Tsumeb, 76
Tsuntsu, 137
Tuffa, 137
Tujuka, 106
Tunis, 71
Tunuka, 115
Turkana, 73
Tushe, 141
Tutu, 108

Ubangi, 73
Ububele, 124, 127
Ububle (f), 130
Ubucwicwicwi, 128
Ubudoda, 136
Ubugotho, 126
Ubuhle, 123, 125
Ubuhle Du, 129
Ubukhosi, 130
Ubukhulu, 125
Ubumhlophe, 130
Ubundu, 77
Ubunsomi, 130
Ubuntu, 127
Ubunye, 135
Ubunzima, 130
Ubuqhawe, 123, 135
Ubuqili, 122
Ubuqotho, 134
Ubusha, 127, 136
Ubusuku, 127
Ubuwozawoza, 123
Ubuzalwane (m), 123
Udade (f), 133
Udalala, 128
Udumo, 87

Uèle, 73
Ugogo, 122
Uhlobo Lomuthi, 124
Ukhozi, 124
Ukhwini (f), 131
Ukona, 127
Ukubekezela, 128
Ukubukisa, 128
Ukuchuma, 130
Ukudikiza, 124
Ukufunda, 134
Ukuhila, 125
Ukuhlangana, 125
Ukuhwalala, 127
Ukukhala, 124
Ukuklaklabula, 124
Ukulalela, 128
Ukulondeka, 132
Ukumangala, 122
Ukuna, 87
Ukuphazima, 135
Ukuphiqilika (f), 86
Ukuqabuka, 131
Ukuqala, 123
Ukuqhama, 130
Ukuqina, 136
Ukuqinisela, 129
Ukuqonda, 135
Ukusindisa, 132
Ukuthembeka, 127
Ukuthembisa, 126
Ukuthula, 87
Ukuthuthuka, 122
Ukuzazi, 132
Ukuzidla, 130
Ukuzihlonipha, 132
Ukuzimela, 126
Ukuzitika, 131
Ukuzwa, 126, 129
Ukwahlula, 135
Ukwindla, 123
Uludumo, 127
Uluhambo, 136
Uluhlonzi, 132
Uluhudo, 87
Ulukhumbi, 134
Ulukloko, 129

Ulunembe, 129
Uluvemvane (f), 123
Uluzime, 123
Uluzwela, 135
Ulwandle, 128, 132
Ulwazi, 132
Umakhi, 123
Umanduleli, 125
Umaphuli, 131
Umarni (m), 138
Umbani, 126
Umbonanhle, 125
Umbuso, 126
Umcabi, 129
Umdlali (m), 134
Umdlalo, 133
Umduze (f), 126
Umenzi, 130
Umfana (m), 123
Umfdlana, 134
Umfelukholo, 127
Umfowethu (m), 86
Umhlaba, 122
Umhlabathi, 124
Umhleli, 128
Umhlola, 128
Umhlwenga, 132
Umholi, 126
Umkhaphi, 129
Umkhosi, 128
Umkhuleki, 130
Umlamuli, 87
Umlingo, 127
Umngane, 86
Umnikelo, 132
Umnotho, 136
Umnyamezele, 132
Umnyelela, 125
Umnyelele, 86, 132
Umnyezane, 136
Umnyuziki, 127
Umoya, 133, 136
Umphathi, 124
Umphezulu, 136
Umphikeli, 124
Umphimbo, 125
Umqambi, 128

Umqondo, 125
Umsayensi, 132
Umshanakazi (f), 87
Umshumayei, 130
Umsindisi, 131, 132
Umsinjwana, 133
Umthala, 125
Umthonyi, 123
Umtshali, 129
Umufo, 125
Umuntu, 123
Umusa, 87
Umvimbi, 123
Umvuzo, 130
Umzalwana (m), 133
Umzukulu, 86
Undlunkulu (f), 133
Undoli (f), 124
Unita (f), 21
Unomuntu, 127
Untanga, 128
Upholi, 128
Usekhona, 122
Usende (f), 129
Ushampeni, 86
Ushukela, 134
Usilika, 133
Utshana, 125

Vaal, 73
Valelisa, 132
Vanessa (f), 40
Varah (f), 5
Varen (f), 5
Varryl (m), 5
Vela, 124
Vernon (m), 29
Veza, 123
Victoria, 73
Vimbeleza, 127
Vindon (m), 8
Virginia (f), 34
Virtue, 6
Volta, 73
Vovovonisa, 131
Vuai, 82
Vuma, 125

Vumela, 135
Vuna, 131
Vusa, 131
Vuselela, 131
Vutha, 125

Wa'azi, 146
Waiga, 89
Waje, 144
Waka, 145, 147
Wa Kiri, 120
Wali, 146
Walinda (f), 3
Wallace (m), 56
Walter (m), 24, 61
Wandah (f), 2
Wandavisa (f), 4
Warke, 142
Warren (m), 54
Warri, 71
Wasa, 142
Wata, 144
Wayo, 139, 147
Wellington (m), 24
Wenday (f), 8
Wesley (m), 48
Whitney, 29, 40
Whoopi (f), 45
William (m), 18,
     24, 32, 36, 41, 61
Willie (m), 61
Willy (m), 61
Wilma (f), 57
Windhoek, 76
Windy (f), 6
Wiwa, 110
Wiwadii, 113
Wiwu, 115
Wolii, 117
Wosan, 108
Wotha, 135
Wplpzo, 101
Wu, 110
Wuta, 141
Wynton (m), 43
Wyomia (f), 58
Wyrone (m), 5

Xerona (f), 55

Yaa Asantewa (f), 64
Yaba, 89
'Ya Mace (f), 88
Yamoussoukro, 75
'Yanci, 141, 143
Yanilenu, 110
'Yantacce, 141
Yanyawa, 141
Yaounde, 74
Yara, 118
Yarantaka, 149
Yarima (m), 145
'Yar'uwa (f), 89
Yasan (f), 67
Yato, 108
Yawa, 136
Yayyafa, 147
Ye, 105
Yetunde (f), 85
Yi, 120, 145
Yin-Logo, 112
Yiwuwa, 145
Yiyara, 119
Yiyitheka, 133
Yohance, 88
Yori, 116
Yunkura, 88
Yvetteen (f), 4
Yvonne (f), 21

Zabalaza, 126
Zaire, 73
Zakara (m), 88, 146
Zaki, 143
Zakiya, 81
Zalika, 82
Zama, 134
Zamani, 144
Zambezi, 73
Zango, 144
Zanko, 139
Zanzibar, 77
Zauna, 143
Zeila, 71
Zetay (f), 8

Zika, 133
Zimbabwe, 70
Zina (f), 58
Zinder, 76
Zindla, 135
Zin-Kibaru (m), 68

Zomba, 76
Zora (f), 34
Zuba, 143
Zuberi, 82
Zuciya, 142
Zuga, 142

Zuila, 71
Zula, 133
Zuma, 137, 142
Zumudi, 140
Zwa, 126, 129

CHILD CARE BOOKS YOU CAN COUNT ON—

from ST. MARTIN'S PAPERBACKS

BEYOND JENNIFER AND JASON
Linda Rosenkrantz and Pamela Redmond Satran
Newly updated, this landmark book is truly the only guide you'll need to naming your baby!
_____ 95444-1 $4.99 U.S./$5.99 Can.

GOOD BEHAVIOR
Stephen W. Garber, Ph.D., Marianne Daniels Garber, and Robyn Freedman Spizman
This comprehensive, bestselling guide lists answers to over a thousand of the most challenging childhood problems.
_____ 95263-5 $6.99 U.S./$7.99 Can.

THE SELF-CALMED BABY
William A.H. Sammons, M.D.
Strung-out babies *can* calm themselves—and this one-of-a-kind guide shows you how to help them do it!
_____ 92468-2 $4.50 U.S./$5.50 Can.